H. M...
121 Cranglea Drive
EH10 5PL

Don't Break
Your Heart!

Don't Break Your Heart!

All You Need
to Know about
Heart Attacks –
and How to Avoid Them

Dr Barry Lynch

Sidgwick & Jackson
London

In association with BBC WALES

First published in Great Britain in March 1987 by
Sidgwick & Jackson Limited
1 Tavistock Chambers, Bloomsbury Way
London WC1A 2SG
In association with BBC Wales

First reprint April 1987

ISBN 0 283 99466 5

Phototypeset by Falcon Graphic Art Limited
Wallington, Surrey
Printed in Great Britain by
Adlard and Son Ltd, The Garden City Press
Letchworth, Hertfordshire

*For my
mother and father*

More than all else,
keep watch over your heart,
since here are
the wellsprings of life.

PROVERBS 4, 23

CONTENTS

ACKNOWLEDGEMENTS

Bob Goosey of South Glamorgan Health Authority first suggested a television series on the prevention of heart disease, and John Stuart Roberts, Head of Television at BBC Wales, encouraged me, and enabled me to make it. The Health Education Council co-produced it with the BBC. This book came out of that series, and I am very grateful to Joanna Edwards of Sidgwick and Jackson and Harry Green, the designer, for their hard work in putting it together.

I am also grateful to Professor John Catford, Director of Heartbeat Wales, who was the adviser on the series and who has read this book and discussed ideas with me. But of course responsibility for the opinions in the book remains mine.

I should also like to thank all those who worked so hard on the television programmes, especially Tom Friswell, Richard Trayler-Smith and Peter Loam, but also Ashley Rowe and Peter Davies (who took some of the photographs in this book), Tim Ricketts, Trevor Simms, Jerry Hoare, Nick Wall, Carl Blundell, David Lowe, Simon Meek, and Philip Croxall.

Finally, my gratitude and affection go to Tessa McKenzie and Tony McAvoy who spent more waking hours with me than I'm sure they care to remember. They made it not only worthwhile but also fun.

PREFACE

The phone call offering me a job at the BBC was interrupted by an insistent high-pitched screech. My cardiac arrest bleep. I apologized and ran.

I was then a junior hospital doctor and, like all my colleagues, spent a great deal of my time treating people with heart attacks and cardiac arrests. Coronary heart disease was routine, the bread and butter of general medical wards.

My attitude to it then is illustrated by the story of a doctor who goes to have a picnic on a river bank. Just as he's sitting down, he sees a drowning man floating down the river. He jumps in, pulls him out, and resuscitates him. Just as he's succeeded, wiped his brow, and felt pleased with himself, he spots another body floating downstream. He repeats his rescue procedure and then sees yet another body. This goes on several more times before another doctor walks past and asks him what on earth is happening. 'Well,' says the first doctor, 'I've been so busy pulling them out and resuscitating them, I haven't had a chance to go and see who or what is pushing them in upstream.'

When I qualified in medicine ten years ago, prevention was very much on the margin of the medical school curriculum (from what I hear, it still is). It is only as I have stood back from medicine that I have seen how lopsided is our allocation of resources and effort. Adequate medical and surgical treatment of existing heart disease is, of course, essential; but more important, by far, is its prevention. Other countries are showing us how vast the scope for such prevention is.

As a medical student, I knew what the risk factors were for increasing the odds of heart disease, but I only realized during the making of the *Don't Break your Heart* television series how impressive was the evidence that an individual could greatly reduce the chance of a heart attack. The realization made me change my own lifestyle: I lost weight, changed my diet, and started exercising regularly.

(Like the great majority of doctors, I was already a non-smoker.)

I hope the evidence convinces you to reduce your risks too. It isn't a quest for immortality: just three score years and ten. Most of my cardiac arrest calls were to men in their forties and fifties. And most of them died.

CARDIFF
The Feast of St Luke the Physician, 1986

INTRODUCTION

A twentieth-century plague

Heart disease is by far the most important health issue in Britain today. Two hundred thousand people a year die from it: more than one person every three minutes. The toll is equivalent to that of a fully-laden jumbo jet crashing every working day, and two of them crashing each Saturday and Sunday. Yet there is no public outcry about it; no calls for a Royal Commission to examine its causes; no cries for the resignation of the Minister for Health.

Heart disease has come to seem a normal, natural way to die. But heart attacks are a mass epidemic and a twentieth-century plague. Their resulting death and disability have crept upon us slowly over the last fifty years, so that someone in middle age dying of a heart attack has now become commonplace. At the turn of this century, Sir William Osler, then the most eminent physician on either side of the Atlantic, could recall seeing only a few dozen cases of coronary heart disease in the course of his long and busy career. Heart disease may have become 'normal' in our society, but it is certainly not inevitable. Everyone in Britain is at risk from a heart attack, but everyone can cut their risk to the absolute minimum.

Heart attacks and death

Heart attacks are not only the main cause of death in this country (more than all cancers put together) but they are also the most important cause of *premature* death (more than thirty times the number of those killed in road accidents). It is often said that a heart attack is rather a good way to die: it's quick, over and done with before you know it. Surely much better than a lingering, terminal illness? Well, a quick heart attack may be all right in your eighties but one man in five in this country will have a heart attack before the age of sixty-five and for half of them it will be fatal.

Sudden death is the most dramatic, but not the only, manifestation of heart disease. Another one man in ten aged under sixty-five will suffer distressing disability from heart disease: either shortness of breath or crippling chest pain.

Heart disease in perspective

'Deadly virus will kill or maim 1 in 5'. One can imagine the mass hysteria provoked by such tabloid headlines if a rampant virus were discovered that took the same toll of pre-retirement-age men as heart disease.

In fact, one doesn't have to imagine it, because the reaction to AIDS is an example of it. But even the gloomiest predictions of the spread of AIDS forecast that by the end of the decade there will be twenty thousand cases of it in Britain. Heart disease will still be by far the most important public health issue.

The heroin problem is also scattered regularly across our front pages. It causes a tragic loss of young lives: about 200 a year in this country. That's only a fraction of the lives cut short by heart disease every day.

To think about heart disease in this way may seem sensationalist: but the figures *are* sensational. Heart disease has very little news value, because it isn't caused by a recently-discovered virus or by a socially-unacceptable and illegal drug. Also, it's not new; heart attacks have been around for a long time. But heart disease is far more contagious than AIDS: we 'catch' from each other the view

The figures *are* sensational

that the sort of lifestyle which leads to a heart attack is normal. And the socially-acceptable, legal substances that we put into our bodies every day – either in our food or through cigarette smoke – are as dangerous as heroin. They certainly kill more people.

Deaths from AIDS and heroin can be prevented. The risk of a heart attack can be greatly diminished too – if you have the will. You cannot be protected from heart disease by a vaccine and doctors alone can't prevent it – but you yourself can reduce your risk to the very minimum.

Britain: the sick man of Europe

In terms of heart disease, Britain is not only the sick man of Europe, but the sick man of the world. Death rates from heart disease in Scotland, Northern Ireland, and Wales are now the highest in the world; England is only just behind her sister nations.

Until recently, heart disease in Britain had been steadily rising: by three per cent in men and ten per cent in women in the last fifteen years. Now the increase in deaths seems

British lifestyle is dangerous

to have levelled off and among some groups in the last couple of years there has been evidence of a very slight decline. That seems good news – until it's set beside what has happened in other countries in the last fifteen years.

Heart disease deaths have shown a dramatic reversal in countries broadly comparable in lifestyle with Britain over that time:

- in the USA down by 37%
- in Australia down by 35%
- in New Zealand down by 30%
- in Canada down by 26%

Similar trends have happened in Finland, Norway, Belgium, Japan, and Israel. This decline in deaths has affected all people in those populations, no matter what their age. In other words, young and old people are at less risk of a heart attack.

Of course, there have been improvements in the medical and surgical treatments of heart disease over this period. But Britain has made similar medical and surgical advances and the decline has happened in countries with differing systems of health care and varying approaches to treating heart disease.

It isn't doctors and hospitals who have been responsible for these dramatic falls in heart-disease deaths. The explanation is that the people in those countries have changed their lifestyles in ways which have made them less at risk of a heart attack.

Compared with countries which have reduced their rates of heart attacks, we in Britain exercise less, we smoke more, and we get more of our food energy from fat, especially animal fat.

Of course, people here are now becoming aware of the message that the average British lifestyle is giving us the highest rate of heart-attack deaths in the world. But we're still not doing enough to change it.

In the next five years we could look forward to the same decline in deaths from heart attack that we've seen in other countries. If we did enjoy even that success (and their rates are still falling) we would save 70,000 lives a year. One of them could be yours.

HEART FACTS

In Britain 1 person dies of a heart attack every 3 minutes: 200,000 a year

★

More than 1 in 3 Britons will die of a heart attack, yet our great-grandparents had scarcely heard of the disease

★

More people in Britain die of heart disease than of anything else

★

1 in 5 men in this country will have a heart attack before the age of 65. Half of them will die

★

Other countries have cut their heart-attack deaths by up to 37% in the last 15 years; in Britain, death rates have hardly changed

★

70,000 lives a year would be saved if we were as successful as people in other countries in tackling heart disease

CHAPTER 1

What is Heart Disease?

There are many different types of heart disease. There are congenital malformations affecting babies and young children, often causing them to be blue and breathless. Adults are sometimes affected by disease of the heart valves, the valves linking the various chambers of the heart together. Then there are various disorders affecting the rhythm of the heart, and others affecting the heart muscle. But all these forms of heart disease are comparatively rare. By far the most common heart disease is the one we're considering: coronary heart disease or CHD. This is the disease of the blood vessels supplying the heart muscle, which is the underlying cause of a heart attack. It is coronary heart disease which has become the mass epidemic of our age and which is largely preventable.

How the heart works

The heart is a bag of muscle the size of a large clenched fist which beats about seventy times a minute. It is surrounded by our two lungs and together they fill the whole of the chest cavity.

With every breath we take, air is drawn into the lungs, which are sponge-like and soak up the oxygen in the air. This is then dissolved in the blood which suffuses the lungs. This oxygen-rich blood is drawn into the heart, which pumps it through the arteries to all the tissues of the body where the oxygen is released in order to keep each cell alive. Blood with the oxygen taken out of it then drains through the veins back to the heart and is pumped again to the lungs to be replenished with oxygen – and so the cycle continues. The heart is a pump; but it has to be a very efficient one because in one day it pumps about 7,000 litres (over 7 tons) of blood.

The heart itself, like any other tissue, needs oxygen to keep it alive. It sends blood to the rest of the body through the main artery, the aorta. Leading off this are tiny arteries – the coronary arteries – which branch out and supply the oxygen-rich blood to the thick muscle of the heart itself. These tiny arteries are responsible for keeping the heart alive. It is disease in them that causes a heart attack. (See colour illustrations 1 to 6.)

Disease in the coronary arteries

Disease in the coronary arteries is caused by a gradual narrowing of these arteries. The culprits are fatty substances in the blood, including cholesterol, which act like an oil-slick. These fats get deposited in the wall of the artery.

At first, there are just little streaks of this fatty material on the wall, but gradually, over the years, these enlarge and affect the whole wall, beginning to narrow the channel going through the artery. This furring-up of the arteries is called arteriosclerosis, which literally means hardening of the arteries. The fatty material which builds up is called atheroma, from the Greek word for porridge. At post-mortem examinations it can be scraped out as a sludge-like substance. (See illustrations 7 to 10.)

Starting early

It has been estimated that over ninety per cent of the adult population suffer from this narrowing of the coronary arteries, to a greater or lesser degree. The frightening thing is that the furring-up process can begin in childhood. Fit young adults who die from accidents have been shown commonly, at post-mortem examinations, to have the fatty streaks beginning to build up in their arteries. Studies of American soldiers (average age twenty-two years) showed that a third or more already had narrowing of the coronary arteries. Heart disease isn't a bolt from the blue; the foundations for it begin in youth. So we all need to be concerned not only about our own coronary arteries but also about our children's. We can do something to keep our arteries clear, and perhaps even begin to reverse the furring-up process.

Angina

Once narrowing of the coronary arteries has occurred, less blood is reaching the heart muscle – and, therefore, less oxygen. If the narrowing is very severe, enough blood may be reaching the heart for it to function at its normal rate, but when it has to work harder – for example, during running or walking uphill – the heart muscle doesn't get enough blood for it to cope with the increased work-load. (See illustrations 11 and 12.) It then sends out a pain signal: a cry of help, for more oxygen or less work. This pain signal is angina, the Latin word for 'gripping' or 'strang-

The heart is surrounded by the lungs, **1**. Although it is situated on the left-hand side of the chest, pain coming from the heart is usually felt in the centre of the chest, over the breast-bone.

With every breath, air is drawn into the lungs, which are sponge-like and soak up the oxygen. Blood suffuses the lungs, picks up the oxygen and is drawn back into the heart before being pumped through the arteries around the body, **2**. (The arteries are shown in red and the veins in blue.) Oxygen-depleted blood then drains back through the veins to the heart, **3**.

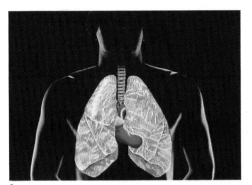

1

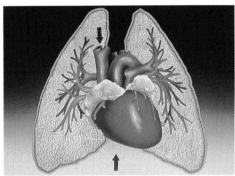

3

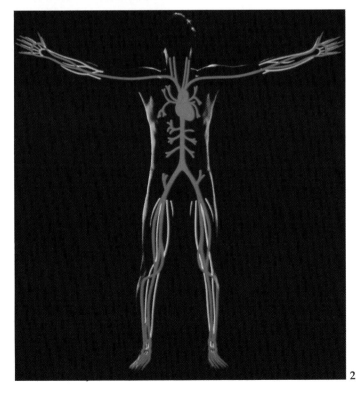

2

The deoxygenated blood that has drained from the body is pumped by the heart back into the lungs in the direction shown by the blue arrows, **4**. The blood is replenished with oxygen and is drawn back into the heart in the direction shown by the red arrows, **5**.

The blood is kept in continual flow by the pumping action of the thick heart muscle, which itself needs to be supplied with oxygen-rich blood to keep it alive and functioning. The arteries supplying the heart are known as coronary arteries, illustrated here as the small branches connecting to the main central artery, the aorta, shown in red in cross-section, **6**.

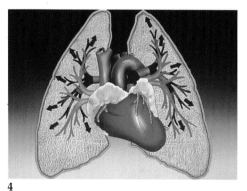

4

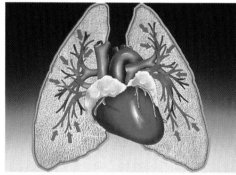

5

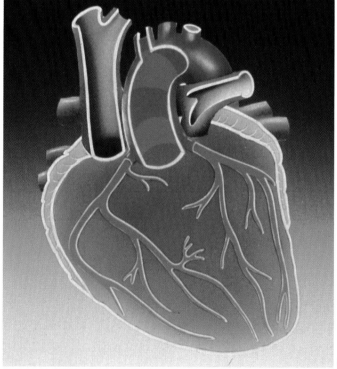

6

The cross-section diagram, **7**, shows blood flowing along a coronary artery. The yellow smudges represent the fatty substances, like cholesterol, which are carried by the blood and are laid down in the artery wall.

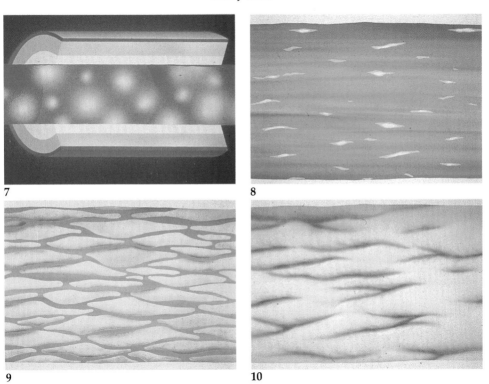

7 8

9 10

At first, there are just little streaks of this fatty material, called atheroma, in the artery wall, **8**. Over a period of years these streaks enlargen until they coalesce and cover the wall, **9**. The deposit then thickens and narrows the blood channel through the artery, **10**.

In the cross-section diagram, **11**, the atheroma has severely narrowed the inner channel of the coronary artery and blood flow along the artery is restricted. Usually, the same furring-up process happens in all the coronary arteries simultaneously, so that the whole heart gradually receives less and less blood and oxygen, **12**. When the heart muscle is called upon to do extra work – for example, during running or walking uphill – the narrowed arteries cannot deliver enough blood to cope with the extra load. The heart sends out a pain to the body. This is angina.

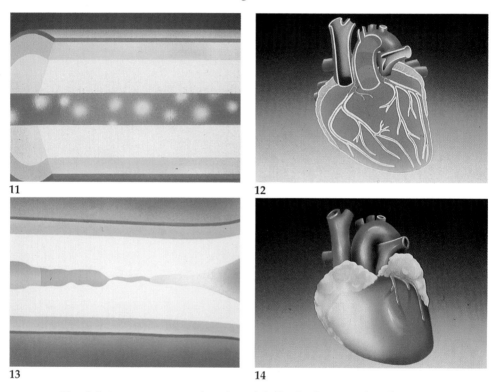

11

12

13

14

Blood clots are a necessary function of the body; for example, when we cut ourselves they prevent us bleeding to death. But in this situation they are dangerous. When the channel of the artery is narrowed and the inner wall roughened by the atheroma, an unnecessary blood clot may be activated. As the clot is carried along the artery it can stick in a very narrow section, **13**, thus stopping the blood flow and causing this section of the heart muscle to die, **14**. This is a heart attack.

ling'. This, in fact, is how people usually describe angina – as a gripping or tightening feeling in the chest, behind the breastbone, though it is sometimes described as a weight or pressure on the chest.

Pain from the heart is usually central, not on the left side as one might expect, though the pain is often felt as going to the left shoulder, or down the left arm, and even to the fingers. It also sometimes radiates up into the neck or jaw. Angina is similar, though usually much less severe, than the pain of a heart attack, and it tends to fade away after a few minutes rest. So, the characteristics of angina are:

- gripping feeling of pain in chest
- central pain, possibly radiating to left shoulder, arm, neck or jaw
- pain quickly eased by rest

In people whose coronary arteries are narrowed, angina may be brought on by:

- exertion, such as going uphill, running, and sometimes even walking quickly
- excitement or anger

Angina is exacerbated by:

- cold weather
- a heavy meal

Angina may be relieved by:

- pausing from whatever exertion brought it on
- tablets, which work either by reducing the heart's work-load and its need for oxygen, or by increasing the amount of blood flowing to the heart
- heart surgery in some cases

People with angina usually know how far they can walk before the angina starts, and they often find they can't walk as far in the winter. Many people live for years with angina, but once this narrowing of the coronary arteries has occurred, there is a higher than average risk of a heart attack. It is vital for people with angina to follow all the guidelines given for reducing the risk of a heart attack.

A heart attack: the causes

Narrowed, furred-up coronary arteries are the foundation for a heart attack. The inner wall of the artery is gnarled and roughened by the atheroma, so there is a greater danger of a blood clot occurring. In the blood are special cells, platelets, which are responsible for its clotting normally – for example, if we cut ourselves. These cells may

'I do love my heart. I want it to work a bit longer!
I mean, I've enjoyed forty-five fantastic years of
good health and a great career and it has got
something to do with the centre of my body,
hasn't it? So I do plan to look after it. I've always
thought, funnily enough, even before I really got
into being conscious of health and fitness, that if
you could break the fifties barrier and not have a
heart condition you've got a chance of surviving
the rest of the years without dying of a heart
attack. You read so much about younger men,
people of my age, thirties to fifties, who have
heart conditions.'

CLIFF RICHARD

become activated as they rub on the rough artery wall and they then release threads, which wrap together and trap other blood cells in them to form a clot or thrombosis. (Hence 'coronary thrombosis' or 'coronary' is a synonym for a heart attack.)

This clot may be carried by the blood flow along the artery until it gets bigger, or meets a narrow section and jams in the artery, stopping all blood flow along it. The section of muscle of the heart served by that artery has its blood supply cut off and dies (see illustrations 13 and 14), and a severe pain signal is sent out. ('Myocardial infarction' is another synonym for a heart attack: the myocardium is the heart muscle and infarction means a cut-off in the blood supply.) If the victim survives the heart attack, the patch of dead heart muscle is replaced by scar tissue.

Sudden death from an attack

Many heart attacks don't even announce themselves in a severe chest pain, but rather in instantaneous death. In such cases, the clot may form higher up the artery so that a great deal of heart muscle has its blood supply cut off, and the heart can no longer function.

At other times, the clot may form at a place which affects

It's all over in a few seconds

the electrical conducting system of the heart, the system which sends out tiny electrical pulses to the heart muscle and causes it to beat rhythmically.

Sometimes a clot hasn't formed at all; it is just that the coronary arteries have become so narrow, and so little blood is getting through them to the heart muscle, that the electrical conducting system stops working properly, the rhythm becomes irregular, and the heart stops beating. It's all over in a few seconds.

Nearly half of all heart attacks are fatal, and of those who do die from a heart attack, half are dead within fifteen minutes. Even the best-equipped and -staffed coronary care unit can't help them because the victims wouldn't reach it in time.

Symptoms of a heart attack

- central chest pain
- feeling faint or dizzy
- sweating
- looking grey and ashen
- feeling sick or actually vomiting
- breathlessness

A central chest pain is *the* first-rank symptom of a heart attack, and all the other symptoms of a heart attack may or may not be present. As with the pain of angina, it's usually felt immediately behind the breastbone or sternum. It is crushing and vice-like in nature, often described as feeling like a heavy weight on the chest. It may radiate down the left arm (occasionally the right arm) and to the fingers. Or the radiation may be to the shoulder, to the neck, into the jaw, or into the back.

Classically, the pain is severe and people know that something serious is wrong. Sometimes, though, the pain is much less severe and people describe it as 'indigestion'.

A crushing and vice-like pain

'Indigestion' felt in the chest, and coming out of the blue, is always suspicious and may turn out to be angina or a heart attack. Sometimes people take antacids for this 'indigestion' for a couple of days before it is discovered that it's really a heart attack.

Whether severe or not, heart pain is seldom sharp or stabbing in nature, and is not usually felt over on the left-hand side of the chest.

What can doctors do?

In the last twenty years there have been advances in the medical treatment of coronary heart disease. There is now a range of drugs which can treat angina; there are drugs which can correct abnormal heart rhythms; and there are drugs which may reduce the risk of someone who's had one heart attack having another. Coronary intensive-care units are now the norm in district general hospitals. More recently there have been advances in the surgical treatment of heart disease.

Coronary artery bypass grafting

This operation was pioneered in Texas in 1964. It's usually carried out on those who have severe angina which is not relieved by tablets. Before surgery, dye is injected into the coronary arteries and X-ray pictures of the heart's circulation are taken. (This is called 'coronary angiography'.) By examining the X-rays it is possible to see the points where a coronary artery is badly diseased, narrowed, or blocked. The surgeon then takes a piece of vein from the leg and sews it to the coronary artery on either side of the blockage. This restores blood flow down that artery. Several grafts may be done at the same time.

Coronary artery bypass grafting is very successful in treating angina: it relieves pain in over ninety per cent of patients. But surgery is, of course, expensive and only about 5,000 of these operations are carried out in Britain each year (compared with 110,000 in the United States of America).

Coronary angioplasty

This is a newer and much simpler procedure than artery bypass grafting, and the results are still being evaluated. It dosn't involve an operation as a tube or catheter is introduced into the heart through the blood vessels. It is guided, under X-ray control, into the coronary arteries and, at the narrrowed section, a balloon surrounding the catheter is blown up and pushes the artery's wall outward, restoring its normal width.

Heart transplants

Heart transplants are carried out for a number of different heart conditions, including very severe coronary heart disease. The cost, in money and resources, of carrying out heart transplants is so great, though, that they could never become common for the treatment of coronary heart disease.

Surgery
is not
the
answer

What doctors can't do

This increase in medical and surgical knowledge and skill has saved many lives. But the number of lives saved has been small compared with the toll of deaths.

- there is no drug which can prevent heart disease
- coronary care units can only hope to decrease deaths by 4% or 5%
- not every case of heart disease is suitable for surgery

Surgical treatment, anyway, hasn't been shown to decrease the death rate from heart disease significantly. But even if surgery were the answer, it would be impossible to carry out 200,000 operations a year. Ninety per cent of the population has unhealthy coronary arteries. Surgery and heart transplants can only have a tiny effect on the margins of the problem, and the highest of high-tech medicine cannot help the fifty per cent of heart-attack fatalities which occur within fifteen minutes. Prevention is not better than cure; it is the only cure.

HEART FACTS

90% of adults in this country have disease of the coronary arteries

★

1 in 3 men in their early twenties have narrowed coronary arteries

★

The furring-up process in coronary arteries begins in childhood

★

Nearly half of all heart attacks are fatal

★

Of those who do die, half are dead within 15 minutes, before medical help can reach them

★

Improved coronary care units would only reduce deaths from heart disease by 4% or 5%

CHAPTER 2

GAMBLING ON YOUR LIFE: THE RISKS

If having a heart attack or avoiding one were just the luck of the draw, then we in Britain would seem to be very unlucky people. Mere chance does not explain why we have climbed to the top of the heart-attack deaths league, while other countries have cut their death rates so much. Of course, for some people the odds of having a heart attack may be higher if they come from a family which is predisposed to heart disease. But that can't explain the massive increase of heart disease in this century, and the dramatic falls in incidence now being seen in other countries. Most of us decide the odds of a heart attack for ourselves.

Risky living

Few people think they live dangerously. They don't go hang-gliding or rock-climbing. They drive with due care and attention to avoid being one of the 6,000 people who are killed each year in road accidents. But 200,000 people die of heart disease. At least a third, if not half, of them

Thirty times more deaths than in road accidents

could have avoided that fatal heart attack by not living dangerously. Smoking, eating too much of the wrong food, obesity, lack of exercise, and high blood pressure will cause more deaths each year than a generation's worth of road accidents.

We're all at risk

One of the ways of preventing a disease is to identify those individuals who are likely to get it and target them in your prevention strategy. But the problem in this country is not that a few people have an extremely high risk of heart disease (though they do) but that the whole population has a needlessly high risk of a heart attack. An *average* lifestyle in this country carries a high risk of heart disease: hence the present epidemic. This is a difficult idea to accept,

An *average* lifestyle carries a high risk

because the commonly-held view is that what the majority do must be right and eating a high fat diet, smoking, and taking little exercise have come to be accepted as normal. Becoming overweight as you get older also seems normal. The *average* level of blood cholesterol in this country and the *average* blood pressure lead to an increased risk of a heart attack. But these average values would be regarded as abnormal in other countries.

Unlike other public health campaigns – for better sanitation, and for cleaner air, for example – this campaign won't only succeed by the actions of government or health authorities, though there is a great deal more a government could do to help:

- ban all cigarette advertising and increase the tax on tobacco
- bring in a full system of food labelling
- reduce the subsidy on dairy products
- change the meat carcass grading system to encourage farmers to produce leaner carcasses
- encourage GPs to do more to prevent heart disease

But heart disease will only cease to be an epidemic when the majority of people choose to live a healthier life.

How great is the risk?

No one can predict exactly which horse will win the Derby but the system of betting in horse-racing depends on the favourites winning most of the time. No one can tell you with certainty whether or not *you* will have a heart attack. But it is possible to assess who is likely to get one.

By considering the 'risk factors' (see p. 26), you can assess your own 'form' and decide whether or not you are in the running for a heart attack. It's highly likely that you are at some risk, and that you'll see the ways you can reduce that risk.

An individual may be greatly at risk of a heart attack and yet may avoid one, of course. We all know of the apocryphal figure who smoked forty cigarettes a day and lived till he was ninety. People do take risks like that and get away with it – but they are very few and far between. Perhaps this tiny minority does have some built-in protection against the various risks. But most of us have no such protection and we're susceptible to the risks. After all, ninety-year-old heavy smokers are a great rarity; heart-attack victims in their forties and fifties are a tragic commonplace.

'I had a father who smoked about sixty or seventy cigarettes a day and for the last twenty years of his life he couldn't walk from one side of a room to the other without having to sit down. Every time I weakened I looked at my dad and thought that's what you're heading for if you keep on.'

ROGER DALTREY

Risk factors

A risk factor is an individual characteristic in a person which increases his or her risk of a heart attack. Some of the risk factors – the decisive ones for most people – are under our own control; others are not. The risk factors for heart disease that we can control are dealt with in separate chapters and the others we'll look at in more detail in this chapter.

- age
- sex
- family history
- diabetes
- use of oral contraceptives
- soft drinking water
- **high blood pressure** (*see chapter 3*)
- **high blood cholesterol level** (*see chapter 4*)
- **smoking** (*see chapter 5*)
- lack of exercise (*see chapter 6*)
- obesity (*see chapter 7*)
- stress and personality (*see chapter 8*)

Of all of these, the three major risk factors, which operate independently of others, are high blood pressure, high blood cholesterol and smoking. These exert their effect no matter what the level of the other risks may be.

Age

The furring-up of the coronary arteries begins in childhood and continues throughout life, so the risk of a heart attack becomes greater with each passing year. The people who get heart attacks in middle age have accelerated the process, invariably by the way they have lived their lives. The process can be slowed right down by taking action on all the risk factors under our control.

One of the other reasons that heart disease increases with age is that, in this country, the *average* blood pressure rises with age. But this is not a normal process, and there are things we can do to stop it happening (see chapter 3).

The risk of heart disease has risen for all age groups in this country and that means that the risk of a heart attack for a man aged forty now is the same as the risk was for a man aged sixty in the 1930s.

Sex

A man in his late forties is five times more likely to have a heart attack than a woman of the same age. Female hormones help protect women from heart disease until they reach the menopause, when women begin to catch men up and their risk of a heart attack becomes almost the same.

Heart disease in women has been increasing, though, and in the last twenty years there has been a rise in heart attacks in women in their thirties and forties. All the same risk factors apply to women as well as men so that their lifestyle can still increase the risk of a heart attack.

Family history

Coronary heart disease often seems to run in families. The risk of a heart attack is increased if a parent or sibling has, or had, coronary heart disease, especially at a young age. However, there is no gene for a heart attack, so what we may inherit is increased susceptibility to the other risk factors and it's all the more important that we reduce all our risks to a minimum.

Unhealthy lifestyles run in families

There's another reason, unconnected with heredity, why heart attacks run in families. Our lifestyles are affected by our parents' lifestyles, and our views of what a normal diet is, whether or not it's normal to take regular exercise, or to smoke, are influenced by our upbringing. If you have a relative who died of a heart attack, consider what avoidable risks they had for the disease.

Diabetes

Diabetes accelerates the furring-up process in the coronary arteries, so men and women with diabetes are more at risk of a heart attack, particularly those who require insulin injections. However, there's evidence to show that where the diabetes is well controlled then the risk is reduced. Again, if you do have diabetes, it's all the more vital that you cut down on every other possible risk.

Oral contraceptives

Oral contraceptives are an effective and acceptable method of contraception for many women and the risks associated with their use are very small. However, women who take oral contraceptives, 'the pill', *are* at increased risk of a heart attack. For most younger women, this increased risk is insignificant: heart attacks are so rare in young women, anyway, and it's likely that the risk is lower now than it used to be when contraceptive pills contained higher doses of hormones. For women over thirty-five who are on the pill, and who smoke, the increased risk does become significant, however. Every woman on the pill should definitely stop smoking.

As you get older, the risks from taking oral contraceptives increase and, once you've completed your family, you should discuss with your doctor alternative methods of contraception. All women taking the pill should have their blood pressure taken regularly as, again, high blood pressure and use of the pill combine to bring a significant risk of a heart attack or a stroke.

Soft drinking water Statistically, there is evidence that heart disease is more common in areas with soft water than in those with hard water. In the United Kingdom, deaths from heart disease have tended to increase more in towns that have introduced water-softening. However, the link is still not proven. Even if it were shown to be true, it is a very minor risk compared with all the other things which are directly under our control.

Controlling the odds To a greater or lesser degree, when it comes to deciding whether or not we have a high or low risk of a heart attack, we control the odds. Avoiding heart disease could be compared with winning a game which requires a little luck, but a lot of skill. It's luck – or chance – to a very limited extent that decides who gets a heart attack early in life. To a much greater extent, it's how we play the hand that's been dealt to us that is crucial. Each of us has a different risk of a heart attack; the important thing is to get your own risk down to the minimum.

It's not *just* bad luck

As we have seen, the three key risk factors are high blood pressure, high blood cholesterol level and smoking. Even moderate levels of each increase the risk of a heart attack by two or three times. If you have two or three of these risks, then the overall odds begin to increase even more dramatically: a sinister compound interest comes into play as the risk factors interact with each. So having two of the key risk factors could increase your risk *four* times; having three of them could increase it *eight* times.

The other risk factors under our own control don't so much act independently as by pushing you in the direction of the three key risk factors. So obesity, lack of exercise, and stress may all increase your blood pressure. Those who don't exercise and those who are overweight have higher levels of blood cholesterol than those who do exercise and are of normal weight. Those who feel stress badly may smoke more.

In the rest of this book are chapters on each of these risk factors, and suggestions on how you can assess and cut down your own risk. That may mean altering lifelong habits, but the changes you need to make are achievable. They are not drastic, but they could have dramatic results. It's an extremely good investment: for a small outlay you'll get a handsome return. You should enjoy your normal span of life, and live to see your children's children.

HEART FACTS

6,000 people a year die in road accidents in Britain; 200,000 die of heart disease

★

Decisive risk factors for heart disease are under our own control

★

A man aged 40 now has the same risk of a heart attack as a man aged 60 did in the 1930s

★

The average British lifestyle puts most people in this country at risk of heart disease

★

High blood pressure, high blood cholesterol and smoking each increase the risk of a heart attack by 2 or 3 times. All three together increase the risk by 8 times

CHAPTER 3

BLOOD PRESSURE

Raised blood pressure is one of the major contributors to the risk of having a heart attack. Even moderately raised blood pressure can increase the risk, particularly if you smoke or have high levels of cholesterol in your blood. High blood pressure also greatly increases the risk of having a stroke, as well as several other diseases, including kidney failure. So it is very important to know whether or not you have raised blood pressure. But how many of us have ever had our blood pressure taken, or, if we have, know the result? Doctors have a range of drugs which they can use to bring high blood pressure down, but there's a great deal we can do for ourselves to ensure our blood pressure remains normal, or to bring it down if it is high.

What is high blood pressure?

Blood pressure is the pressure exerted by the heart and arteries to push blood around the body. A good analogy is the water flowing out of a hose-pipe. To increase the water pressure (to reach a distant rose-bush, say) you could either increase the flow at the tap (this is the equivalent of making the heart work harder) or decrease the diameter of the end of the hose-pipe, by partially covering it with a thumb, for example (this is the equivalent of constricting the blood vessels). The water pressure coming out of the hose is the sum of these two pressures, and blood pressure is the sum of the amount of blood being squeezed out of the heart per beat (the 'stroke volume') and the resistance encountered when it squeezes through the blood vessels (the 'peripheral arterial resistance').

The circulation of the blood is a closed system, and if this peripheral resistance increases because the blood vessels don't expand enough to let blood flow through them easily to reach all parts of the body, then the heart has to pump harder to move the blood around and the blood pressure rises. This puts a strain on the heart and it also causes wear and tear on the walls of the arteries, damaging their lining, and making it more likely that they will fur up.

Normal and abnormal high blood pressure

The medical term for high blood pressure is hypertension, which is an unfortunate word because it implies that high blood pressure means a high level of tension. Striving, competitive, impatient people *may* be more likely to develop hypertension than others but, in fact, our blood pressure can be high when we're feeling very relaxed. The most placid people can have high blood pressure.

Everyone's blood pressure rises when they're excited, angry, or afraid. It also rises during exercise. All these are quite normal reactions to mental or physical stresses and this normal rise in blood pressure is brought about by hormones, like adrenalin, which constrict some of the arteries and make the heart work harder. This ensures that more blood and, therefore, oxygen flow to the muscles and

Our blood pressure can be high even when we're feeling very relaxed

to the brain. (It is the so-called 'fight or flight' mechanism so that we can get ourselves out of danger; we have it in common with all animals.) But in the case of all these stresses, the blood pressure returns to normal when the particular stress ends.

High blood pressure, or hypertension, is diagnosed when our *resting* blood pressure is raised; that is, it is high when we're resting, sitting reading, watching television, or sleeping. This is abnormal. We can't feel anything when our blood pressure is high and it very rarely causes any symptoms. The only way to know is to get it measured.

There are rare hormone and other diseases which can raise blood pressure, but most high blood pressure in this country is the result of a range of factors in the susceptible individual – many of which are under our own control.

These are some of the things which may contribute to high blood pressure:

- being overweight
- taking too little exercise
- smoking
- drinking too much alcohol
- eating too much salt and too much fat
- feeling too much stress and being wound up

What is normal?

It's difficult to define what 'normal' blood pressure is, just as it is to define 'normal' height. We may know what 'average' blood pressure is, but there's every reason to suppose that, at least for older people in this country, the average blood pressure is too high, and, in fact, is abnormal.

Blood pressure is expressed as two figures. The first, higher, figure is the 'systolic blood pressure', a measure of the pressure when the heart is actually pumping out blood. The second figure is the 'diastolic blood pressure', the pressure when the heart is filling up with blood between beats.

Blood pressure is always expressed with the systolic first, for example 120/80, or 120 over 80 as it's usually said. The units are millimetres of mercury; the sphygmomanometer which measures blood pressure has a glass column of mercury rather like a barometer. This column is linked to a cuff which is placed around the upper arm. The cuff is inflated until blood flow along the arm's main artery is stopped. The pressure exerted by the cuff is measured by the column of mercury. The air pressure in the cuff is then gradually released while the person taking the blood pressure listens with a stethoscope over the artery at the elbow. Blood begins to flow again down the artery as the pressure in the cuff equals the systolic pressure. A rhythmic sound is then heard through the stethoscope. As the diastolic presssure is reached, the sound becomes muffled.

While 'normal' is difficult to define, it is desirable for your blood pressure to be under 140/90 and preferably 120/80 or less, whatever your age. (It's very very rare to suffer from low blood pressure unless you've just lost about four pints of blood; if you're fit and feeling well, then the lower your blood pressure, the better.)

Even doctors in this country have got used to the idea that people's blood pressure rises with age and this has come to be accepted as normal. It isn't. It's true that it's par for the course for people living in Britain, but there are many societies where it doesn't occur. Among Polynesian islanders for example, who still follow their traditional life, high blood pressure is virtually unknown. There's convincing, and increasing, evidence that it's our lifestyle that is responsible for dangerously increasing average blood pressure in this country. A third or more (perhaps over half) of adults in this country, develop high blood pressure which becomes a threat to their health.

The answers to high blood pressure

Find out what your blood pressure is. The best way to do that is to ask a nurse or doctor to take it. The best GPs are checking blood pressure now as a matter of routine when middle-aged people consult them about something else. In some practices, one of the nurses may give regular blood pressure checks, too. There's no excuse not to as it is quick to do, completely safe, and cheap, and high blood pressure and the diseases that are caused by it can be prevented. The Royal College of General Practitioners recommends

Get your blood pressure measured

that everyone between the ages of twenty and sixty-four should have their blood pressure taken at *least* once every five years. (American doctors recommend every two years.)

So next time you see your GP ask for your blood pressure to be taken. But high blood pressure shouldn't be diagnosed on one reading; three or so readings over a few weeks should be consistently high before 'hypertension' is diagnosed. Do what Americans always do: ask for the actual figures. British doctors are, on the whole, more conservative than American doctors in deciding the level at which someone has hypertension and then in deciding whether or not to give drugs to treat high blood pressure. Their conservatism may be wise, as the drugs can produce side-effects. But there's increasing evidence now of the benefits of treating even 'mild' hypertension. When to give treatment is a matter for your doctor's judgement, as in an individual case there may be various other factors to consider. Your doctor may decide not to give you tablets at all, but to suggest ways in which you might change your lifestyle to bring down your blood pressure.

- cut down your fat intake. A high-fat diet has been shown to have an effect in raising blood pressure (see p. 45)
- cut down your salt intake. In susceptible people, the effect of too much salt in increasing blood pressure can be dramatic (see p. 52)
- don't drink too much alcohol. It pushes up your blood pressure (see p. 54)

'It's very difficult to diet and stop smoking at the same time, but unless you are not going to put on weight too much then it's very important to control your intake of food. Which is what I've done, which is why I now look so slim and beautiful!'

SIR ROBIN DAY

- stop smoking. Smoking increases blood pressure and increases your risk of a heart attack or stroke (see p. 60)
- start taking some exercise – even moderate amounts will help (see chapter 6)
- get your weight down to the ideal weight range for your height (see p. 83)
- learn how to manage stress in your life, and how to relax (see p. 89)

Even if your blood pressure is only slightly raised (e.g. 130/85), you'd be wise to follow the same advice. And, in fact, following the advice if your blood pressure is 'normal' (120/80 or below) should ensure that it stays that way, and doesn't rise with age. The ideal is to get your blood pressure down to normal without tablets, but if your doctor prescribes tablets, do take them. It will mean you cut your risk of having a stroke or heart attack.

HEART FACTS

High blood pressure rarely causes symptoms;
you may have had it for years without knowing it.
Get it measured

★

Even slightly raised blood pressure increases the
risk of a heart attack or stroke

★

The blood pressure of a third (perhaps a half) of
adults in this country is too high

Blood pressure needn't rise with age; it's abnormal
that it usually does so in Britain

★

There's a great deal you can do yourself to keep
your blood pressure normal or to reduce it
if it is high

CHAPTER 4

DIET

Food should be enjoyable; eating well is one of the great pleasures of life. So much health education is full of negative messages: don't eat this; don't eat that; don't eat the other. Sometimes the only positive message seems to be, 'Eat more brown rice'. But, unfortunately, everyone in Britain has slipped into an unhealthy pattern of eating. We need to understand why that has happened so that we can make sense of the advice we're being given.

Moderation is the watchword. Nothing needs to be banned outright, but some of the things you're eating too much of may have to come into the category that Americans call 'sometimes' food. No one wants to follow a set of rules blindly, and to make an informed choice about what we eat we need to know something about the changes in our diet that have happened this century, and to understand something about the scientific evidence that points inescapably to the link between our food and the heart-disease epidemic.

You are what you eat

The connections between our health and our food have been known for centuries, though mostly as a mixture of myth and folklore. Scientific evidence for a direct link was made in 1747 by James Lind, when he discovered that fresh oranges and lemons added to the diet of British sailors both treated and prevented scurvy. His elegant experiments proved the link beyond doubt, even though the missing factor in the sailors' diet, vitamin C, was not isolated and named until much later.

Would that all links between our diet and our health were so easily demonstrated. The problem now is not a dearth of information, but a surfeit of it. And folklore hasn't been pushed aside by the mass of scientific evidence and research. From television, newspapers and magazines we are bombarded with advice about our diet. 'The Pineapple Diet', 'The Hollywood Diet', 'coffee causes cancer', 'coffee is an aphrodisiac', 'doctors agree on what foods can cause heart disease', 'professor says eat what you like'. No wonder most people are confused.

The consensus on changing our diet

The plethora of information and advice does, unfortunately, obscure the crucial point: the scientific evidence of the benefit of making some changes in the way we eat is now overwhelming. In the past, advice was given based on partial or shaky evidence. We have become confused because the advice has seemed contradictory. Eating cheese used to be encouraged because it was a high protein food; now, because of its fat content, the advice is to go easy on it. Bread and potatoes used to be thought fattening; now, we're encouraged to eat more of them if we want to lose weight because such starchy foods fill us up without delivering too many calories.

'International medical opinion is now quite convinced that if we make certain adjustments to the way we eat we can reduce heart disease in the whole of the population. It's a change we all should make in our whole pattern of eating.'

DELIA SMITH

The medical and scientific consensus is now very great indeed. All reputable international reports (over twenty at the time of writing) are broadly in agreement. Of course, by its nature, the scientific evidence is incomplete, but enough is now known, *without doubt*, to recommend important changes in the way we eat. These changes have been endorsed by two recent British government reports, NACNE (the National Advisory Council on Nutrition Education) and COMA (Committee on the Medical Aspects of Food Policy). The changes they recommend are for the whole population, not just for a small section who think they're at special risk from a heart attack. Following the changes will not only reduce the risk of a heart attack but will also reduce the risk of bowel cancer, diverticular disease, diabetes, gallstones, and constipation. You have much to gain.

The changes we need to make

To reduce the risk of a heart attack we need to:

- eat less fat, particularly saturated fat
- eat less sugar
- eat less salt
- eat *more* fibre

Most people have now heard of this basic advice; the problem is making sense of it. You may think, for example, that you already eat little fat or sugar – but we all eat more than we think. We need to understand the advice before we can work out ways of following it.

It is a pity that the advice adds up to three 'don'ts' and a 'do', but these would not involve great changes in the way we eat, and certainly don't mean we have to give up familiar food and eat a faddy diet. If we followed the

Healthy eating need not be boring

advice, we'd go back to the sort of food that our great-grandparents were eating, and that our forebears were eating a hundred years ago, two hundred years ago, and a thousand years ago. Remember that heart attacks are a twentieth-century plague.

There are many people today who live on this healthier

diet. Chinese food follows these principles, as does food of the Mediterranean basin: southern French food, Italian food, Greek food. No one can say that healthy eating need be boring. Of course, if we make some simple changes – and we can do that gradually – good old British grub can be healthy, too. But remember, the *average* British twentieth-century diet leads to a high risk of heart disease.

Our unhealthy pattern of eating

Human beings are classified as omnivores – we eat everything. But the mix of what we eat has changed. Our cave-people ancestors ate mostly fruit, grains, and vegetables, with some fish and, only occasionally, meat, when the hunt had been successful. This diet was low in fat and high in carbohydrates and fibre, and contained a moderate amount of protein of meat, fish and vegetable origin. In the last century, our Victorian forebears ate a diet that had the same sort of balance. Only the really very rich ate meat

Welcome back to fibre!

every day (and they probably accounted for the very rare cases of heart disease). For some people, meat was a treat once a week. Many others saw it perhaps only a few times a year. (Undernutrition, of course, was the main diet-related illness then.)

Since the beginning of this century, and coinciding with the epidemic of heart disease, our diet has changed so that we now eat more fat and less carbohydrate (though vastly more sugar). The amount of protein we eat has remained about the same. Fat has increased because we eat so much more dairy produce and processed food. Carbohydrate has decreased largely because we eat fewer potatoes and less bread. Carbohydrate is a rather slippery term. Sugar is a carbohydrate but it is classed as a 'simple' one; it has been refined so that it is sugar and nothing else (see p. 51). The carbohydrates we have been eating less of (and of which we need to eat more) are complex carbohydrates, starches and fibres which are found in grains, fruit, and vegetables.

Many changes have come about because people have more money to spend on food, and much food has become cheaper. But fashion, and changing ideas of what's good for us, have played a part, too, in altering the pattern of what we eat. Some of the most important changes, though, have come about without anyone – as a consumer – taking any conscious decisions. Our greatly increased consumption of fat and sugar, for example, is also explained by the different ways in which food is now presented to us.

Processing food

Processing food – refining it, subtracting from it, adding to it, mixing it together, and packaging it – has often meant making it cheaper, more nutritious, and more tasty. But there's been a price to pay, too.

For example, when the machine milling of rice was introduced in the Far East it was considered a great advance and people found the resulting polished rice, with the outer husk taken off, very palatable. Unfortunately, the

There's a price to pay for 'convenience'

process caused the disease beriberi. An important vitamin, B1 or thiamin, was present in significant quantities in the outer husk. For people living on a rice-based diet, this was their most important source of the vitamin. By eating polished rice they became vitamin B1 deficient, and that led to the disease.

The beriberi story shows us that our bodies can sometimes be tricked. Polished rice tasted as good as whole rice and it could make you feel as full. There was nothing to show that it was lacking something – until people became ill.

The problem with most processed food today is not that it is deficient in essential vitamins: they're added to some foods (by law to margarine, for example) to make sure we get enough of them. Nor is processed food lacking in nutrients. In fact the opposite is the problem: a superabundance of nutrients, a surfeit of calories. Processing food can cause large numbers of calories to be packed into a small space, because it so often includes those two dangerous 'calorie packers', fat and sugar.

Just think about calories for a moment. We all know that a pound of apples is far better for you than a pound of chocolates. Whoever felt guilty about eating an apple, or two, or three? We know that the number of calories (or energy, or turning-into-fat-ability) of food doesn't only depend on the weight of the food. A pound of apples has far fewer calories than a pound of chocolates. In fact, ten pounds of apples has fewer calories than a pound of chocolates, and that's how our bodies can be tricked. It's (fairly) easy to eat a pound of chocolates at one sitting, but it's almost impossible to eat ten pounds of apples. Whole, natural, unrefined food has a low calorie-to-weight ratio because it's packed with fibre. It's almost impossible to take in too many calories if we eat this type of food because our appetite control centre in the brain will soon tell us 'you're full'. But processed, refined food often has a very high calorie-to-weight ratio so we can take in an enormous number of calories before our appetite centre tells us to stop.

Calorie packers Chocolate is largely fat and sugar. Sugar and fat are notorious for packing a huge number of calories into a small space. Two teaspoons of sugar contain nearly as many calories as a quarter-pound of peas, while one ounce of butter contains more calories than ten ounces of potatoes. This explains how over forty per cent of the calories in the British diet comes from fat. It's not that forty per cent

Watch out for hidden fat

of the *weight* of our food is fat, but, weight for weight, the fat that is there has so many more calories than other food. We also eat more fat than we think, though, and much of it is 'hidden' like in that chocolate.

So many of the products of the food industry rely on sweetening fat, as in chocolate, biscuits, and cakes, or in salting, as in crisps, sausages, and pasties, in order to make them more palatable. A meat pie or sausage may deliver half or even more of its calories in fat. Fat is cheaper than meat.

Filling not fattening The calorie-to-weight ratio also explains why we can *lose* weight by eating more bread, especially if it is wholemeal, and potatoes. Weight for weight, these foods do not contain too many calories, but they do contain bulky carbohydrates, starches, and fibres. This means that we can't eat too much of them, and so consume too many calories, before we get full. They're filling foods, but not fattening foods. They do become fattening when we add fat to them of course: when we fry the potatoes as chips,

We can *lose* weight by eating more bread

and slap butter on the bread, we start bumping up the calories. The same goes for pasta and rice: they are fine until we add fatty sauces.

Fat: the killer

Fat is not only the main culprit in making us fat, it is also the number one suspect in the heart-attack epidemic.

The whole 'fat' issue is complicated. It suits some food manufacturers to keep it that way, so that they can keep making profits out of feeding us with vast quantities of 'hidden' fat. To understand fat, and to make an informed choice as you walk round the supermarket, and read the food labels, you need to know about cholesterol, saturated fat, and polyunsaturated fat, and what effect they have on your health.

The cholesterol story

Cholesterol is a natural substance present in our blood; in fact our body manufactures it and small quantities of it are essential for health. The problem is that virtually everyone in Britain (in common with most other Western industrialized countries) has too high a level of cholesterol in their blood. It's this excess cholesterol which gets laid down in the walls of arteries and contributes to their furring-up. It's not just that only a few people have high levels of cholesterol; the *average* level of cholesterol in this country is so high that it makes the risk of heart disease high for almost the whole population. That's one of the reasons why heart attacks are an epidemic in Britain. The World Health Organization (WHO) has reported that it knows of no country in the world where coronary heart disease is common where there is not also this high *average* level of cholesterol in the population.

It's this rise in the average level of blood cholesterol of

the whole population that seems to have been the trigger that has set off the increase in heart attacks that we have seen this century. All the other risk factors, such as smoking and high blood pressure, then multiply this already greatly-increased risk. For example, in Japan, the *average* blood cholesterol level is much lower than our average. In spite of the fact that the Japanese smoke as much as the British, they suffer from far fewer heart attacks than we do (though, of course, smokers there run the same, huge, risks of lung cancer). There is no in-built mechanism, though, that protects them from heart attacks. It's been shown that when Japanese move to the United States and start to eat a Western diet, then their blood cholesterol levels rise and their risk of a heart attack soon catches up with the average American's risk. This proves that what we eat affects the level of cholesterol in our blood.

'Good' and 'bad' cholesterol

The situation is complicated a little by the fact that there are two different types of cholesterol. The blood carries cholesterol in two ways: as 'good' cholesterol and as 'bad' cholesterol.

'Bad' cholesterol, or LDL-cholesterol (low-density lipoprotein-cholesterol), is laid down in the walls of the arteries and is responsible for blocking them. 'Good' cholesterol, or HDL-cholesterol (high-density lipoprotein-cholesterol), actually helps the body get rid of the 'bad' cholesterol by sweeping it out of the blood. So it is not only the total amount of cholesterol in your blood that's important, it is also the ratio of HDL- to LDL-cholesterol. There are several ways we can increase the good, HDL-

Increase the 'good', decrease the 'bad'

cholesterol and decrease the bad, LDL-cholesterol (see pp. 66, 70 and 83). Overall, of course, we want to decrease the *total* cholesterol in our blood.

The level in your blood

Ask your doctor to measure your blood cholesterol level. Most don't do this as routine but it's reasonable to ask if you have any of the other risk factors. The most accurate measurement is when you have fasted overnight, so if you'd like it done when you go to the surgery, don't have breakfast. Ask your doctor for the actual figures. If yours is over 5·2 millimoles per litre (equivalent on another scale to 200 milligrammes per decilitre) you should aim to reduce it. If it is high, your doctor may suggest an analysis of the good and bad cholesterol ratio.

Saturated and unsaturated fat

What we eat determines the level of cholesterol in our blood. But it isn't just a simple matter of our blood cholesterol rising when we eat a lot of cholesterol in our diet. What matters far more is the total amount of fat we eat, particularly the type of fat that's called 'saturated'.

The amount of saturated fat in our diet has a greater influence in increasing the cholesterol level in our blood than eating 'neat' cholesterol. Our body responds to a high level of saturated fat in the diet by producing a high level of cholesterol in the blood. So, we need to cut down the saturated fat in our diet rather than worry about cholesterol itself. (Egg yolks are one of the biggest sources of the cholesterol that we eat, but we'd have to eat a dozen a day to have any appreciable effect on our blood cholesterol. It's wise to limit intake to three eggs a week, or less, though.) Cholesterol usually occurs in combination with saturated fat, so if we cut that down then we will automatically cut down our cholesterol intake as well.

'I've been thinking much more about diet. I very much like food, but it's very important to try and make the link between healthy food and enjoyable food. It is difficult finding a healthy diet when you're constantly being put in front of meals which are not of your choice, and it's rather bad manners not to look as if you're enjoying it. Since the kind of diet I try to follow is based on low fat, low sugar, and reasonably low salt, you have some problems! Fresh fruit is always a stand-by, nearly everywhere you can find fresh fruit, and people seem to understand. And there's usually chicken.'

THE HON. WILLIAM WALDEGRAVE, MP

How do we detect and cut down on saturated fat? Saturated is a chemical term referring to the state of the hydrogen bonds which link the fat molecule together. Saturated fatty acids, or saturates, are other terms for saturated fats. Polyunsaturated fat (polyunsaturated fatty acids, or polyunsaturates) has a different chemical make-up, with looser hydrogen bonds. The chemical difference between the two types of fat is reflected in their physical appearance: saturates are usually solid at room temperature, while polyunsaturates are liquid. Saturates are mostly found in animal fat, while polyunsaturates are mostly found in vegetable fats, but all the types of fat we eat are made up of differing percentages of saturates and polyunsaturates. Eating saturated fats increases the level of cholesterol in the blood whereas polyunsaturated fats decrease the total cholesterol in the blood. (There is also a group of fats called monounsaturated – olive oil is rich in this kind of fat – which has no effect on the cholesterol in the blood.)

This doesn't mean that we should stop eating saturated fat and only eat polyunsaturates. It is the ratio between polyunsaturates and saturates that is important: we need to redress the balance, and we could do that by cutting down saturates by about twenty-five per cent. It would be impossible, anyway, to cut out saturates, because all fats contain saturates and polyunsaturates, though in differing proportions. For example, the fat in cream is sixty per cent saturated whereas the fat in sunflower oil is less than fifteen per cent saturated. Even the fat in soft margarine, which is labelled 'high in polyunsaturates' is about twenty per cent saturated (if it weren't, it would be liquid).

This type of margarine lists 'hydrogenated vegetable oil'. This means that some of the oil has had hydrogen added to it so the bonds in the fatty acid become 'saturated' with hydrogen atoms and so are 'hydrogenated' and therefore solid. This is fine as long as the percentage of saturates is low (twenty per cent or so), but hard margarine has more of this hydrogenated oil, which means that it can be quite high in saturates. Hydrogenated vegetable oil can also be used to make commercial cakes and biscuits, so again, these may be high in saturated fat. Hydrogenated vegetable oil acts like any other saturated fat: it pushes up the cholesterol in your blood. So 'vegetable oil' doesn't always mean 'healthy'.

How to cut down saturated fat

To cut down on the saturated fat in our diet, we need to know where in our food it is. Most of us would think that we don't eat much fat; how can it be that over forty per cent of the calories in our diet comes from fat?

As we've seen, weight for weight, fat is much higher in calories than carbohydrates and protein. It packs a lot into a small space. Also many of our everyday foods contain more fat than we think and, on top of all this, we eat over four times more saturated fat than polyunsaturated.

According to the government's national food survey the major sources of saturated fat in our diet are:

- cream, milk and cheese (about ¼)
- meat and meat products (about ¼)
- butter and margarine (about ¼)
- oils and cooking fats (about ¹⁄₁₀)
- crisps, chocolate, snacks etc (about ⅙)

The consistant recommendations, both by the WHO and the two recent British government reports, are that we should cut down the total amount of fat in our diet and, in particular, cut down the amount of saturated fat in our diet by at least *a quarter*. In order to make it easier to do this, we can substitute some polyunsaturated fats for the saturated fats that we're cutting down on, but overall we still need to cut down greatly on our total fat consumption. So if we look again at where most of the saturated fat in our diet comes from, we can begin to think about how to reduce it.

When thinking about this whole question of fat it is important to consider how all the average figures apply to you and your family. If you never eat cream that doesn't mean that you're not getting your dose of saturated fat

'The thing about a lot of recipes is that they are meant for special occasions, not for everyday. As long as you eat healthily, you can still enjoy some special recipes from time to time, and hopefully you will still reduce the risk of heart disease.'

DELIA SMITH

from somewhere else (perhaps you eat chips fried in lard several times a week). If you never eat cream or chips, perhaps you regularly eat cakes and biscuits (five per cent of the saturated fat eaten in this country is in biscuits). On *average* everyone in this country is getting over forty per cent of calories from fat (half of which is saturated).

Remember that nothing need be absolutely banned – moderation is the watchword. If your life wouldn't be worth living without chocolate biscuits then you'll have to think about some other ways in which you personally are going to cut down the fat, and sugar, in your diet. The important thing is not so much individual items, but the total amount of fat that you eat. Only you know where that fat is coming from, but here are some guidelines to help you discover where all that fat getting inside your arteries and furring them up is coming from and how to start fighting back.

Cream

Cream contains very large quantities of fat and, together with milk and cheese, makes up about a quarter of the total fat in our diet.

- double cream is 48% fat
- whipping cream is 35% fat
- single cream is 18% fat

Cream is very definitely in the category of 'sometimes' food. Of the fat it contains, two-thirds of it is saturated. Whether or not it's a significant contribution to your overall intake of fat depends, of course, on how much cream you eat. The ideal is to cut it out completely, or just to have it as a very occasional treat.
    Instead of cream you can try:

- low-fat yoghurt, which is much less than 1% fat
- Greek-style yoghurts, which taste much creamier than natural low-fat yoghurt, but are 8-10% fat
- low-fat soft cheeses like Quark and fromage blanc or fromage frais. (This latter comes in tubs of 1% and 8% fat varieties and is an excellent substitute for cream.)

Milk

It might seem odd that milk is an important supplier of fat in our diet. 'Ordinary', full-fat (silver top) milk is about four per cent fat, two-thirds of which is saturated. The total amount of fat might seem quite low, but it's important to consider not only the percentage of fat in a particular food, but how much of that food we consume. If we drink just less than a pint of milk a day – six pints a week – then we would be consuming as much fat as in half a pint of double cream. Even half a pint a day is the equivalent of drinking nearly a pint of single cream a week. We need to cut down the amount of fat we get from milk, but that doesn't necessarily mean drinking less milk. You can change to:

- semi-skimmed milk (red and silver top). This has *half* the fat of ordinary milk

How much fat food contains

Adults should not eat more than about 80 grams of fat a day. (The exact figure varies from one person to another.) The figures below show how many grams of fat there are in some foods.

meat and meat products		roast potatoes	8g
individual meat pies		**chapatis**	
pork pie	30g	paratha	22g
steak and kidney pie	24g	chapati (made	
¼lb burger	20g	with fat)	10g
sausages *(2 large)*		**cheese** *(60g)*	
ordinary	21g	stilton	22g
low-fat	11g	cheddar	19g
pork chop		camembert	13g
fried with fat left on	25g	edam	13g
grilled with fat left on	20g	low-fat cheddar	9g
grilled, fat removed	8g	cottage cheese	2g
mince *(1 serving – 85g)*		**spreads** *(10g portion)*	
ordinary cooking	14g	butter or margarine	8g
with fat poured off	6g	low-fat spread	4g
roast chicken *(1 serving – 85g)*		**milk** *(1 pint)*	
with skin	12g	full-fat	22g
without skin	4g	semi-skimmed	11g
bacon *(1 serving – 60g)*		skimmed	1g
streaky, fried	25g	**cream** *(1 serving – 30g)*	
streaky, grilled	20g	double	13g
liver *(1 serving – 60g)*		whipping	10g
fried	8g	single	6g
stewed	6g	**sweet snacks**	
fish		small bar chocolate	15g
cod *(1 serving)*		halva	11g
fried in batter	9g	2 digestive biscuits	6g
steamed	1g	**savoury snacks**	
3 fish fingers		1 samosa	26g
fried	11g	small bag of crisps	
grilled	6g	ordinary	9g
potatoes *(1 serving)*		low-fat crisps	7g
thin-cut chips	17g	Chinese pastry with	
thick-cut chips	8g	bean filling	6g
oven chips	7g		

By courtesy of the Health Education Council

- skimmed milk (blue and silver top). This has virtually no fat at all, so it's perfect for greatly reducing your fat intake while continuing to drink milk, but it's thinner than full fat and so takes a little getting used to.

One point to stress: skimmed and semi-skimmed milk have the same amounts of protein and calcium as full-fat milk. In fact, nutritionists would say they become even more nutritious because you're getting more goodness per calorie.

Cheese Cheese can contain a lot of fat, and again, that fat is two-thirds saturated.

- cream cheese is 50% fat
- cheddar-types are 33% fat
- camembert and brie are 23% fat
- cottage cheese is 4% fat

You should go for a lower-fat cheese like one of the soft French cheeses rather than cheddar. (The reason for their lower fat content is that they are soft, i.e. they contain more water, and so contain less fat and fewer calories ounce for ounce.) There are now low-fat cheddar-type cheeses available, which are only about fourteen per cent fat.

Meat and meat products Meat accounts for a quarter of the fat in our diet and could be adding a significant amount of saturated fat to it. Of course, the amount of fat depends on the cut of meat, but even lean meat can contain significant amounts of fat.

- roast shoulder of lamb is 26% fat (leg is less fatty)
- roast leg of pork is 20% fat
- grilled rump steak is 12% fat
- lamb and beef fat are about half saturated; pork rather less than half

You should cut down on the number of times you eat red meat and, when you do have it, choose lean cuts with as little visible fat as possible. In place of some red meat you should eat more:

- chicken, which has less fat, which is less saturated (if you take the skin off you more than halve the fat)
- fish, which is a very good source of protein without much fat. The fat is low in saturates and oily fish, like herring and mackerel, are high in polyunsaturates
- meatless meals. You don't need meat or fish for protein

If you 'pair' the vegetable foods listed below you will get all the essential amino acids, the building blocks of protein, that your body needs, and end up with a complete protein meal. Pair beans, or peas, or lentils, or nuts with rice, or wholemeal bread, or pasta.

Try to reduce your intake of all 'made-up' meat products: meat pies, pasties, sausages, salami, and pâtés. These tend to be very high in fat as fat is cheaper than meat and can be mixed with it to stretch it. Remember, half the calories in a sausage may be fat; nearly two-thirds of the calories in a meat pie may come from fat. It is best to eat meat you can identify.

Butter and margarine

Butter is about eighty-two per cent fat, of which two-thirds is saturated. Margarine is about eighty per cent fat, and, depending on the type of margarine, twenty to forty per cent of this fat is saturated. Together they make up a quarter of our fat intake.

- switch to a margarine labelled 'high in polyunsaturates' or 'high in essential polyunsaturates'. (Margarines not labelled in this way contain significantly more saturates and there is less advantage in switching to them from butter.)
- try the newer low-fat spreads (some of these contain half the fat of butter or margarine)
- if you continue to use butter, spread it as thinly as possible

Oils and cooking fats

Aim to switch from saturated fats to polyunsaturated fats and try to reduce some of the oil or cooking fat you use. It accounts for one-tenth of our fat intake. All oils are a hundred per cent fat; lard is about ninety-nine per cent fat.

- in lard about 50% of the fat is saturated
- in corn oil, groundnut oil, olive oil, and soya oil only about 20% of the fat is saturated
- in sunflower oil, and safflower oil only about 15% of the fat is saturated

Obviously, the less saturated fat an oil contains the more polyunsaturated fat it contains, so look for, and use, one of these 'named' oils rather than lard or blended cooking fat. Beware of oils just labelled 'vegetable oil'; it is possible these could contain the cheaper palm or coconut oils, which are unusual amongst fats of vegetable origin in having very high percentages of saturates.

When you fry potatoes to make chips, they absorb a lot of fat. You can halve the amount of fat by cutting the chips thickly and frying them quickly in hot oil. Again, use an oil low in saturates and high in polyunsaturates. If you re-use the polyunsaturated oil, however, it will gradually become saturated, so it is best to shallow-fry in new oil.

Don't forget that grilling food rather than frying it significantly cuts the fat content.

Snack and convenience foods

These foods account for one-sixth of our total fat intake, which might seem surprising. But crisps and other salted snacks, chocolates, biscuits, cakes, and all manufactured pastry products are high in fat. This fat is often high in saturates, though it can be difficult to tell from the label. If you do eat these foods, you can dramatically cut your fat (and sugar) intake at a stroke by ceasing to do so. At the least, you should reduce your consumption. You could try instead unsalted nuts, fresh fruit, carrots, celery, and dried fruits like figs, dates, and apricots.

Fat and the heart

Remember that by cutting down your intake of saturated fat, and increasing the proportion of polyunsaturated fat in the fat you do eat, you will reduce the level of cholesterol in your blood. This in turn means that your coronary arteries will be less likely to fur-up and so your risk of a heart attack will decrease.

Eat less sugar

Can you believe that you eat a hundredweight of sugar a year? On average, we eat two pounds of sugar each a week in this country – as much as people in the last century ate in a whole year. Half of the sugar is out of a packet and we add it ourselves to food; the other half is in manufactured foods. Obviously sugar is added to fizzy drinks and sweet confections, but it is also added to breakfast cereals, sauces, chutneys, and tinned vegetables. If you start reading the labels on food, you'll be surprised where sugar is shown as an added ingredient.

It is not that excess sugar is especially bad for the heart, but it is an important reason why so many of us are overweight. In nature, sugar comes bound up with fibre – as in fresh fruit, for example. As fibre is bulky and filling, it's impossible to eat large quantities of sugar when it's combined with fibre. In the manufacturing process sugar is refined and concentrated, and we can eat a large quantity of it before we feel full.

Sugar is often described as containing 'empty calories'. It has no nutrients whatever – just calories – and it is a myth that you need sugar for energy: all food can be converted by your body to energy. It is also a myth that brown sugars are better for you than white; they're not – sugar is sugar. Molasses, glucose, dextrose, honey, and syrup, all amount to the same thing – sugar. By cutting back on sugar, we can cut down on calories without losing any nutrients.

- read food labels. The ingredients are listed in weight order with the main ingredients first. Avoid processed food high in sugar
- avoid breakfast cereal with added sugar: it can double the calories

- cut down on manufactured confectionery, chocolate and sweets
- eat fresh fruit more, instead of puddings
- buy tinned fruit in natural juice rather than syrup
- cut down the sugar in your recipes
- wean yourself off sugar in tea and coffee
- the ideal is to reduce your sugar intake by half

Eat more fibre

Fibre is a carbohydrate found in all vegetable matter. It used to be called 'roughage'. We don't digest fibre, but it is an important part of the food we eat because it helps the digestion process and keeps our bowels working properly. As we've been increasing the amount of processed foods we eat, the quantity of fibre in the national diet has gone down. This decrease in fibre consumption has been associated with a range of diseases including bowel cancer, constipation, gall-bladder disease, and diabetes. If we increase the amount of fibre in our diet it will – among other beneficial effects – reduce the amount of cholesterol in the blood, and give us a feeling of fullness without too many calories.

Fibre is found in all fruits, vegetables, cereals, and pulses in varying quantities, but they all contain some and the following are particularly good sources. You should try to increase the amounts you eat of all these types of food:

- wholemeal bread (white bread contains some fibre, too, but only about a quarter of the quantity of wholemeal) – four thick slices a day is a good minimum
- whole potatoes (that is, baked or boiled in their jackets)
- wholegrain breakfast cereals
- all kinds of beans, and peas and sweetcorn
- dried fruit and nuts
- rice, especially brown rice
- pasta, especially wholewheat pasta
- lentils and other pulses
- leafy vegetables like spinach

Fibre and the heart

Remember that increasing the amount of fibre in your diet will help to reduce the level of cholesterol in your blood and so decrease your chance of a heart attack.

Eat less salt

We all eat far more salt than we need – perhaps ten times more. On average we eat about half an ounce, or twelve grams, a day – that's two whole teaspoonfuls. As with

Fibre-rich foods

Adults should try to eat at least 30 grams of fibre a day. The figures show how many grams of fibre each item has.

bread (4 slices)		yam	3g
wholemeal bread	11g	leeks	3g
brown bread	6g	dahl	3g
white bread	3g	sprouts	2g
breakfast cereals		swede	2g
(1 serving)		**fruit and snacks**	
2 Weetabix	5g	2 dried apricots	7g
2 Shredded Wheats	5g	1 banana	3g
Puffed Wheat	4g	raisins (30g)	2g
unsugared muesli	4g	unsalted peanuts (30g)	2g
porridge	3g	1 apple	2g
cornflakes	3g	**spaghetti** (1 serving)	
vegetables and beans		wholemeal	6g
(1 serving)		ordinary	2g
red kidney beans	10g	**potatoes** (1 serving)	
peas	7g	baked in jacket	3g
baked beans	6g	boiled with skin on	3g
spinach	5g	boiled without skin	1g
sweetcorn	5g	**rice** (1 serving)	
plantain	5g	brown	3g
lentils	4g	white	2g
carrots	3g		

By courtesy of the Health Education Council

sugar, however, we don't completely control the amount of salt we eat. The biggest part of our salt intake is not what we add in cooking or at the table, but what is added by manufacturers to processed food.

This abnormal level of salt intake is thought to be partly responsible for so many people in this country having high blood pressure. Some of us are sensitive to this unnecessary salt and it pushes up our blood pressure. The safest thing, therefore, is for us all to reduce our salt intake. It would be almost impossible not to get enough salt – even if we ate no salt and no processed food with salt, we'd still get about double our needs from the salt that occurs naturally in food.

We've trained ourselves to like the taste of salt and to think that food doesn't taste of anything if we don't add it. But we can retrain our palates and it is surprising how quickly they can adapt. Once we begin to appreciate the natural tastes of food, then salted food begins to taste rather nasty.

● read food labels. Again, you'll be surprised where salt is added to food

- look for products marked 'low' or 'no added salt'. Tinned and packet soup is often high in salt and stock cubes can be very salty
- use less salt in your cooking. Herbs and spices, lemon juice, and mustard can be used instead of salt to add flavour
- don't add salt to food without tasting it first – you should aim eventually not to have a salt cellar on your table
- cut down crisps, salted nuts, and other salty snacks
- cut down on foods with a great deal of added salt, like bacon

Any salt is salt: sea salt crystals may be more aesthetically pleasing but they could still have the same effect on your blood pressure. Salt substitutes contain other chemicals like potassium chloride (salt is sodium chloride) as well as salt, they're expensive, and it's much better to retrain your tastebuds.

Alcohol

Alcohol isn't usually regarded as food, or part of our normal diet, but for many people it can be a significant part of their energy intake. Remember that it can pack in a large number of calories. Cutting your alcohol intake can help to reduce your blood pressure if it's high, and sticking to a moderate intake can help ensure your blood pressure remains normal. (The mechanism of how alcohol increases blood pressure is not known, but it has been confirmed in several international health surveys that people's blood pressure rises as the amount of alcohol they drink increases.)

There are plenty of other health reasons why you should only drink in moderation, of course. What is moderation? Half a pint of beer, a single measure of spirits, a small glass of sherry or port, and a glass of wine all contain the same alcohol content. This amount of alcohol – a 'standard drink' – can be used to measure your own alcohol consumption.

- men should not drink more than 21 standard drinks a week, that is about 3 a day
- women should not drink more than 14 standard drinks a week, that is about 2 a day

There is some statistical evidence that *moderate* drinkers are at less risk of a heart attack than either teetotallers or heavy drinkers. This assertion is still controversial, though, and you should remember that increased drinking may bring other health risks. Drinking in moderation, as defined above, seems to be safe for most people.

HEART FACTS

There is a direct link between unhealthy eating and heart disease

★

Over 20 international reports now agree that the diet most people eat in this country is unhealthy

★

The heart-disease epidemic coincides with the addition of more fat and sugar to our diet since the beginning of the twentieth century

★

On average, we each consume over 40% of our calories in fat

★

Much fat and sugar is 'hidden' in processed foods – the consumer has no choice

★

We should cut our saturated fat consumption by at least a quarter

★

Saturated fat pushes up the level of cholesterol in the blood; polyunsaturated tends to reduce it

★

More fibre in our diet helps to reduce the cholesterol in our blood

★

The *average* level of blood cholesterol in Britain is so high that we are all at risk of clogged arteries

CHAPTER 5

SMOKING

Everyone knows that 'smoking can seriously damage your health', but few realize how great the risk is of being killed by cigarettes.

Smoking is associated, of course, with lung cancer. Virtually everyone who dies of lung cancer is, or was, a smoker; it's extremely rare in non-smokers. Cancer is the second commonest cause of death in Britain after heart disease and the toll of death from lung cancer is enormous. Lung cancer is the most common cancer in men and is about to overtake breast cancer as the commonest cancer in women. Smoking is associated, too, with cancer of the mouth, of the throat, of the larynx or voice box, and of the oesophagus. These are urgent and compelling reasons not to smoke.

But far more smokers are killed by a heart attack than by cancer. Smoking seriously damages your lungs; but even more seriously, it damages your coronary arteries. Most heart-attack victims in young middle age are smokers.

Risks of smoking

The increased risk of a heart attack if you smoke is phenomenal and the evidence for this increased risk is indisputable. In Britain, the most important studies have been done on doctors over the last thirty years.

The first link between smoking and lung cancer was made in 1948, and that between smoking and heart disease in 1951. As the evidence linking smoking and premature death accumulated, British doctors began to stop smoking in large numbers. As they did so, their mortality rate began to fall compared with other British men of the same age; in other words, they began to live longer. Similar studies have been done all over the world with the same results: when people stopped smoking, they began to live longer than smokers.

These studies have shown that, for men aged thirty to fifty-nine, smoking twenty or more cigarettes a day more

*'Three or four weeks after smoking, I suddenly noticed
I was breathing properly. My lungs were nice and clear and
I thought, if
I hadn't
smoked during
the whole of
my career,
who knows, I
might have
played an
extra couple
of years.'*

BOBBY CHARLTON

than *trebled* the risk of heart disease. When the figures for the British doctors' study are broken down into different age groups, the results are even more dramatic. The study considered men who smoked twenty-five or more cigarettes a day:

- those under 45 years of age are *15* times more likely to die of a heart attack than non-smokers
- those aged 45–54 years are three times more likely to die of a heart attack than non-smokers
- those aged 55–64 years are twice as likely to have a fatal heart attack

These figures certainly don't mean it's safer to smoke as you get older; the total number of heart attacks increases in older age groups as other risk factors – age itself, high blood pressure, high blood cholesterol levels, lack of exercise and so on – come into play. But the smoker always more than doubles his risk, whatever his age.

The increase in risk of a heart attack from smoking is also directly linked to the number of cigarettes smoked. Even five cigarettes a day significantly increases the risk for all age groups; twenty cigarettes a day trebles the risk;

'Once I smoked a hundred in a day and I felt so disgusted, such contempt for myself. They are smoking you, you're not smoking them. Then for about three days, every time I reached for a cigarette a feeling of revulsion came over me as I remembered the hundred. After about four days I suddenly realized I hadn't had a cigarette for four days – and I hadn't gone without a cigarette for four days since I was thirteen, you know. But I don't feel any withdrawal symptoms, I don't feel any twitching, I don't want to put my hand round anybody's throat – and I haven't had a cigarette from that day and I haven't wanted a cigarette since that day.'

DENNIS NORDEN – *writer and broadcaster*

and forty or more cigarettes a day increases the risk *twenty times*. In addition, a heart attack suffered by a smoker is more likely to be a fatal one.

Those who smoke a pipe or cigars don't have the same risk as cigarette smokers, but their risk is increased compared with non-smokers. The type of cigarette smoked doesn't affect the risk, either; mild, low-tar brands carry just the same increased risk of a heart attack as others.

The *good* news is that a smoker who stops smoking reduces his risk of a heart attack from the first day without cigarettes. After a few years, his risk of a heart attack is down to what it would have been had he never smoked.

The lady killers

Much of the research into heart disease refers to men because they are more likely than women to die in middle age of a heart attack. But over the last fifteen years in

Britain, rates of heart disease have risen faster in women than in men. (Women still have far fewer heart attacks, and the rates may now be beginning to level out, and even fall slightly in some groups.)

These figures reflect the fact that women are smoking more cigarettes than they used to. Overall, the number of

'Suddenly I realized that I was committing suicide. All you've got to do is believe that it's killing you and then it's not relaxing.'

ESTHER RANTZEN

women smokers has been falling, though the number of teenage girls who are smoking is rising. Those who do smoke are smoking more, however. Among other effects, it seems smoking may bring on earlier menopause, causing women to lose the protection their hormones give them against heart disease (see p. 26).

If older women who are using oral contraceptives smoke, they dangerously increase their risk of a heart attack (see p. 27).

There is also another incentive for women not to smoke: the babies born to women who do smoke have a lower birth weight. There are some indications that this retarded growth in the womb may continue to affect children as they grow up. Babies of smoking mothers are also more likely to develop pneumonia in the first year of life.

Smoke gets in your heart

The idea of smoking harming your lungs is easy to visualize: the smoke goes directly into the lungs and so does its damage. How it damages the heart is less easy to picture. As well as tar, cigarette smoke contains about 2,000 chemicals. Some of these chemicals remain in the lungs, but others are absorbed into the blood and can then be carried to the heart and thence to the rest of the body, including the brain. Two of these chemicals, at least, have a direct effect on the heart: nicotine and carbon monoxide.

Nicotine, which reaches the brain seven seconds after first inhaling cigarette smoke, is responsible for the addictive nature of cigarettes. Nicotine is a poison. It is more toxic than arsenic or cyanide and can be used as an insecticide. The amount of nicotine contained in twenty or thirty cigarettes and injected as a single dose into the bloodstream would be fatal. Nicotine constricts the blood vessels, particularly the coronary arteries, and so reduces the amount of blood reaching the heart muscle; at the same time it increases the heart's need for oxygen. It raises blood pressure, increases heart rate, and may cause irregularities in the heart rhythm.

Carbon monoxide – the gas in car exhaust fumes – combines with the haemoglobin in the blood more easily than oxygen. The effect is to push oxygen out of the blood as it becomes replaced by carbon monoxide. So blood reaching the body's tissues – including the muscle of the heart – is carrying less oxygen for their needs.

The effects of nicotine and carbon monoxide happen after smoking just one cigarette. The insidious, cumulative effect of cigarette smoking is that it accelerates the furring-up process of the coronary arteries. Cholesterol is laid down in the inner walls of the arteries faster in smokers than in non-smokers. Once the coronary arteries have

'Giving up smoking is a tough struggle, but you can do it. I did it: it was very hard but I did it and I'm glad I did it. I'm richer and healthier, and I'm alive!'

SPIKE MILLIGAN

become diseased, the effect of cigarette smoking is even more ruinous and the total effect is that the heart has to work harder and harder on less and less oxygen.

But that's not all: cigarette smoking activates the platelets in the blood to become more 'sticky' (see p. 17), and so, having laid the foundation of the heart attack, makes the end stage, the formation of the blood clot or the thrombosis, more likely, too.

Risks for passive smokers

So far we've only been considering 'active' smoking, the effects of cigarettes on the smoker. Research is increasing into 'passive' smoking, the effect of cigarette smoke on non-smokers who have to breath smoke-polluted air. 'Mainstream' smoke is the smoke that is drawn through the cigarette into the smoker's lungs; 'sidestream' smoke is the smoke coming off the end of a lit cigarette and going into the atmosphere. Sidestream smoke contains higher concentrations of some chemicals than mainstream: five

'My small son wrote to me saying: "Dear Dad, if
you don't stop smoking your lungs will look like
this." And there was a picture of what they might
look like. "Don't be a clot, Dad, give it up now,
yours sincerely," and he'd signed his full name,
and I was quite shaken by this letter.'

PAUL EDDINGTON — *actor*

times more carbon monoxide and four times more
nicotine.

Non-smoking spouses of those who smoke twenty or
more cigarettes a day have an increased risk of lung cancer.
Children of smokers are more likely to suffer from asthma
and chest infections, too. But smokers are doing even more
damage to their children's health. Children are more likely
to start smoking if they have a parent or parents who
smoke because they will see smoking as normal behaviour.
Heart disease is catching!

How to stop

Ten million people in Britain have stopped smoking and
you can join them, but you need to have the confidence
that you can do it. What follows is just one suggested plan
for how to stop.

Decide to stop

The decision to stop is crucial. No one else can nag you
into it — you know how counter-productive that is. But
why do you get annoyed when people go on at you to stop
smoking? If you're honest with yourself it is partly because
of the guilty feelings you have about smoking. Very few
smokers want to continue to smoke; most want to stop.
Once *you* have decided to stop, you're halfway there.

- think of the reasons why you personally want to stop
  smoking and write them down
- for example, your husband or your wife may want you
  to stop; you may want to save all the money you're
  wasting on cigarettes; you may be worried about your
  children's health; you may want to prove to yourself
  that you are in charge of your own body
- which are the most powerful reasons? Which will you
  think about to stop you from wavering from your
  decision?
- calculate how much you spend on cigarettes every

'I coughed all the time, I coughed all night, I couldn't go to the theatre without coughing, and I was in quite a bad way. I can't remember how many I actually smoked, or the amount it cost. All I know is that by stopping smoking I saved the equivalent of a gross-income increase before tax of several thousand pounds a year.'

SIR ROBIN DAY

week, every month, and every year. Write it down. Promise yourself that when you give up you'll buy yourself something you want with the money you'll save

Prepare to stop
- choose a day about two weeks away when you will stop – perhaps at the week-end or when on holiday
- put two elastic bands crosswise around each cigarette packet you use – having to take off the elastic bands makes you think about each cigarette you smoke
- don't accept a cigarette from others
- as you smoke each cigarette, don't do anything else. Smoke it quickly and concentrate on your senses, your taste and sense of smell.
- concentrate on smoking the cigarette. Think about the effect the cigarette is having on your body
- change brands twice a week – preferably to a milder brand each time
- keep a 'smoking diary' (it only need be a piece of paper). Every day, write down the time you had a cigarette. Write down how important that cigarette was to you. Was it associated with anything (like having a coffee, or chatting to a friend)? How easily could you have done without that cigarette? Fold the piece of paper and tuck it into the elastic bands on the cigarette packet, so that you write something each time you reach for a cigarette. Write before you smoke. (By using this diary, you'll see which your 'key' cigarettes are, and where you'll have to be on your guard when you stop. Think of ways you'll avoid these situations or overcome them.)
- get a large glass jar and put all your cigarette ends for the two weeks into it. Look at it each time you smoke.
- don't carry a lighter or matches on you

- tell your family and friends you're going to give up. You may be surprised how helpful they are
- ask your smoking friends not to offer you cigarettes from now on. You may find friends who are ex-smokers particularly helpful; smoking friends may scoff (remember they probably want to give up, too)

Stop
- as soon as you wake on the chosen day, tell yourself you no longer want to smoke. Read your reasons again
- give yourself a treat. Buy something for yourself or go out for a meal. Promise yourself further treats with the money you save by not smoking
- be alert for withdrawal symptoms. You may get sleepy or become restless and irritable. But many people get no withdrawal symptoms at all
- if you do get a craving for a cigarette, tell yourself you're in control now, not the nicotine. Time the craving; you'll find it will only last a few minutes

'All the sort of things I'd been told in life about how bad it was for me didn't make much sense until I really knew in myself that that's what I wanted to do.'

GERALDINE JAMES – *actress*

- if the urge to smoke is very strong, deal with it by taking a quick walk, doing some gardening, chewing a pencil, eating an apple or carrot, chewing gum, brushing your teeth or taking a shower
- think of other ways which will work for you – perhaps some deep breathing. Take a big breath, and then let it out very slowly. You may find it helpful to repeat to yourself 'I do not want to smoke' as you breathe out

'I do feel so much better. I'm extremely vain and I think that I actually look better: my eyes are clearer, my skin's clearer. I wake up in the morning and my mouth doesn't feel filthy and for my singing I can breathe much better. When I stopped smoking I didn't put on an ounce because I was watching; I suppose I was being very careful.'

LULU

- be on your guard, especially at the times you know will be more difficult. Use the ways you've thought of to distract yourself. If you always smoke at the end of a meal, for example, get up from the table straightaway and go and do something else
- list the advantages you're gaining by not smoking
- look again at how much money you'll save
- tell yourself at the end of the day that if you can manage one day without cigarettes you can manage through the rest of your life. You're going to take one day at a time, and your first day has been successful

Staying stopped

- tell yourself at the beginning of each day 'I don't want to smoke', and read your reasons for being a non-smoker
- remember you're taking one day at a time. As each day goes by without a cigarette, you're building up an investment. Don't throw it away
- make sure you're not tempted to accept 'just' one cigarette from someone. One leads to another and another
- if you do have one cigarette, don't feel you've failed. Think of how you're going to resist the temptation next time
- start exercising regularly. You'll feel more relaxed and less tempted to have a cigarette
- avoid social situations where you smoked, for a few weeks. When you've had a few drinks, you'll be easy prey for the temptation to smoke
- keep adding to your list of advantages: your breath smells fresher; you can taste your food more; your clothes don't smell of stale tobacco smoke; you're in charge of your own body
- one month, and then one year, after you've stopped smoking, buy yourself something with the money you've saved

---

Even after a year, remember you could get hooked again. Don't be caught off your guard by accepting even one cigarette

---

Stop-start-stop Don't feel a failure if you do go back to cigarettes. Two-thirds of ex-smokers say they find it easy, but some people do find it difficult. Everyone can do it, though. Remember, ten million people in Britain are ex-smokers, and many of them gave up more than once before they finally succeeded.

10 million
Britons
are ex-smokers

Try again as soon as you can. You'll know quite a bit about how to stop by now. Write down what happened last time, and think of ways you'll stop it happening again. Though you've lost one battle, be determined to win the war.

The benefits of stopping Apart from all the apparent and immediate benefits of stopping smoking, there are hidden and even greater benefits.

- your risk of a heart attack will start to reduce from day one
- your heart will be getting more blood and more oxygen and will be under less strain
- your blood will be less liable to clot
- the furring-up of your coronary arteries will slow down
- the total level of cholesterol in your blood will decrease, and the ratio of 'good' HDL-cholesterol to 'bad' LDL-cholesterol will increase (see p. 43)

Excuses for not stopping Looking at some of the common excuses for not stopping, and seeing why they are valueless, might also help you stop, or stay stopped.

- 'I'll put on weight'. It's a myth that everyone who stops smoking puts on weight, though some people do. Whatever weight you did put on, however, would be a small risk to your health compared with the risk of smoking. (You'd have to put on about 10 stone to equal the risk of smoking twenty cigarettes a day.) But you needn't put on any weight at all if you're careful; if you do find yourself hungrier when you stop smoking, try snacking on non-fat, non-sugary foods like fresh fruit and vegetables. Taking exercise is going to stop you gaining weight, too

- 'I'll be impossible to live with'. Some people do get irritable when they give up smoking, but it usually passes after a few days. Anyway, think of what you're inflicting on your friends now as they have to inhale your cigarette smoke. They'll bear a few days of grumpiness if it means you're going to be healthier and live longer

- 'I've given up before and I got a cough and sore throat'. Some people develop a cough after giving up smoking. It's a natural reaction: your lung's defence systems begin to work again and they bring up all the muck that's been deposited in them by cigarette smoke. Others develop a sore throat in the first few days after stopping. This is because cigarette smoking has been irritating your throat, but it's also been numbing it. A slight discomfort means your throat is returning to normal

- 'I'll lose my only pleasure in life'. You know this is phoney – ask anyone who's given up smoking. You'll feel fitter and fresher and won't want to go back to cigarettes. And the extra money can bring you new pleasures!

Other ways of helping you stop

People find many different ways useful and helpful in stopping smoking – mine is just one suggestion. Acupuncture and hypnosis help some people, though you usually have to pay for them. Your local health authority, or even your health centre, may run anti-smoking courses. Your GP will know of any in the area. Your GP will also give you encouragement and advice and may decide to prescribe nicotine chewing-gum, which has been shown to be

---

'I'm not going to smoke any more. Irrespective of anything else ever again. I am now a non-smoker for life. Now I can't give up can I? I can't go back on my word.'

DAVID SUCHET – *actor*

---

effective in helping people to stop smoking. Unfortunately, it's not available on an NHS prescription so you'll have to pay for it – but it's much cheaper than smoking. Don't waste your money on advertized 'magic cures' to stop smoking.

In the end, though, it comes back to your own willpower. You don't need an extra special iron will to succeed, but you do need to make the definite decision that you will succeed. Then you'll do it.

HEART FACTS

Most heart attack victims in young middle age are smokers

★

For men aged 30–59 smoking trebles the risk of heart disease

★

Male smokers under the age of 45 are 15 times more likely to die of a heart attack than non-smokers

★

40 or more cigarettes a day increases the risk 20 times (and mild, low-tar brands carry the same risk as others)

★

Having stopped smoking, the risk of a heart attack reduces from day one and within a few years is down to that of a lifelong non-smoker

CHAPTER 6

EXERCISE

Taking regular exercise can't guarantee that you won't get a heart attack, but it will certainly cut your risk. There is plenty of evidence now to show that those who take regular exercise are less likely to get a heart attack than those who don't; and if they do get a heart attack, it will probably be milder and less likely to be fatal. Those who do not exercise regularly are more than twice as likely to get a heart attack as those who do.

Evolution and exercise

The human body is made to exercise regularly. Our cave-people ancestors had to do so: they ran and climbed in order to hunt and gather food. We may live in a push-button world, in which we don't even have to leave our armchairs to change television channels, but our bodies are not adapted for it. They were designed for vigorous activity, and our joints and muscles – especially our heart – miss it. If we don't exercise, our bodies are like badly-tuned engines; they don't work efficiently. It's no surprise, then, that our arteries start clogging up.

The benefits of exercise

Regular exercise gives so many bonuses:

- it will set you up for the day; you'll feel better, work better, and have more energy
- it will help you sleep better and more soundly
- it's a very good way of relieving stress; those giving up smoking will find it particularly helpful
- it will help to keep your joints and muscles in good working order right into old age
- it will strengthen your bones, so that there'll be less risk of osteoporosis, or thinning of the bones, as you grow older
- it will improve your circulation so that more oxygen will reach all parts of your body

'Exercise is very important.
I get less time to do it now than I used to for all the obvious reasons, but it's a release, it's a freedom, it's a good way to work out all kinds of frustrations. Perhaps for that reason I ought to do it more. You feel better for yourself. It is true — fit body, healthy mind.'

RT HON. NEIL KINNOCK, MP

- it will cause the percentage of fat in your body to go down, from an average of 22% in non-exercising men to 16% in exercising men and from an average of 30% in women who don't exercise to 20% in those who do
- it will help you to maintain or achieve your ideal weight

Most important of all, though, are the bonuses it gives you in the fight against heart disease:

- it will help ensure that your blood-pressure remains normal, or help to lower it if it is high
- it will help to build up the strength of your heart so it can do its normal work effortlessly and have a bigger reserve capacity
- it will decrease the total level of the cholesterol in the blood, increasing the 'good' HDL-cholesterol while decreasing the 'bad' LDL-cholesterol (see p. 43)

- it will, therefore, help to prevent the laying down of the fatty deposits in the heart's arteries
- it will, in other words, help you to become biologically younger than non-exercising people of the same age

What sort of exercise?

Any kind of exercise is better than none and if you've not exercised for a long time, you should take it easy at first. For the heart to get maximum benefit though, your exercise needs to be:

- aerobic
- regular
- vigorous

Aerobic exercise

All exercise which uses your large muscles (that is, the muscles of your legs and arms) rhythmically is aerobic, especially when you're moving your body over the earth's surface or through water. It's called 'aerobic' because when your large muscles start moving in this way, they need oxygen, so you will need to breathe more deeply to take it

'I'm generally very aware that it's good to get out of breath as regularly as possible in which-ever fashion suits you best, really.'

KIM WILDE – *singer*

in and your heart needs to pump faster to deliver it. This tunes up your lungs and heart and, eventually, they can do this work with less effort and you have a greater reserve capacity.

Examples of aerobic exercise are:

- brisk walking
- running or jogging
- running on the spot
- swimming
- climbing stairs
- cycling
- using a stationary exercise bike
- rowing
- tennis (especially singles)
- energetic dancing
- squash

Some of these are considered in more detail later.

Anaerobic exercise is 'static' and doesn't get the large muscles moving rhythmically. Examples of this are weight-training and taking part in a tug-of-war. It's good for strength and body-building, but it's not enough on its own to get you fit. And it doesn't give your heart the benefits that aerobic exercise does.

Regular exercise

The recommended amount of aerobic exercise to reduce the risk of heart disease is three sessions a week, each lasting at least twenty minutes, ideally without stopping. Again, anything is better than nothing and you may find it easier to do just two sessions of half an hour. Remember, though, that three twenty-minute sessions would be much more beneficial than one one-hour session in a week. Of course, if you can exercise every day it would be excellent. It's wise, though, to give your body a rest at least one day a week from vigorous and energetic exercise.

Vigorous exercise

The exercise needn't be strenuous, but it must be vigorous enough to get you puffing and out of breath. You shouldn't be so out of breath, though, that you couldn't carry on a normal conversation. And vigorous exercise shouldn't be uncomfortable or produce tightness or pain in your chest, or neck, or arm. You have a built-in monitor which tells you whether or not you are getting the right amount of exercise for your age: your pulse rate. As you exercise, your heart rate goes up to supply extra oxygen to the muscles. The rate is a good guide to whether you're exercising vigorously enough to give your heart some benefit, or whether you're exercising too strenuously and should slow down. If you're unfit, you'll be able to get your heart rate up to a profitable speed just by walking.

Take your pulse (on the thumb side of the wrist or at the neck, beside the windpipe) for ten seconds immediately after you've exercised, and multiply it by six (to give the rate for a minute). If your pulse is faster than the safe maximum for your age (see below), you need to take it more easily. If it's below the minimum rate needed for benefit to the heart (also see below), you can afford to be more vigorous. You'll soon get to know what's right for you and won't need to keep checking your pulse. If your pulse is irregular, or if you do get pain in the chest, you should see your doctor.

The minimum rates for benefit to the heart, and the safe maximums, taken during or immediately after exercise, are:

- age 20-29 – 140/minute (min.),   170/minute (max.)
- age 30-39 – 130/minute (min.),   160/minute (max.)
- age 40-49 – 125/minute (min.),   140/minute (max.)
- age 50-59 – 115/minute (min.),   130/minute (max.)
- age 60-69 – 105/minute (min.),   120/minute (max.)

Excuses, excuses

Anyone can think of a dozen excuses not to exercise but none of them holds water.

- 'I'm too fat'. Being overweight is an excellent reason to *start* exercising because it will help you to lose weight. Of course, you need to take it slowly at first, but you'll soon begin to feel the benefit. If you're embarrassed about exercising with people, begin with an exercise you can do in the privacy of your bedroom, like running on the spot, skipping, or using a stationary exercise bike
- 'I'm too old'. You're never too old to exercise. Of course, as you get older, you can't exercise as vigorously, but as

'I think that it's very important to keep up with a fair degree of exercise. I always feel that in the days that I do swim I get through the day much better from having had a swim first thing in the morning. It's a very good way of waking you up and toning you up for the rest of the day.'

RT HON. DAVID STEEL, MP

long as you're puffing a little, you're getting the maximum benefit. Regular exercise will also help ensure a more active old age
- 'I'm too tired'. Regular exercise will make you feel less tired. You'll find you have a lot more energy and will also begin to sleep better
- 'I've got medical problems'. Most people, even older people, don't need a medical check-up before starting regular exercise. Some American doctors would say you need a medical check-up if you *don't* exercise.

'You need a medical check-up if you *don't* exercise'

Obviously, if you're unfit, it's wise to take it slowly and gently at first, and you should consult your doctor first if you've suffered, or are suffering, from any of these conditions, or are worried about any other aspect of your health:

- high blood pressure or heart disease
- chest problems like asthma or bronchitis
- back trouble or a slipped disc
- joint pains or arthritis
- recuperation from illness or an operation.

In all these conditions, the right exercise will help you to be healthier, but it's wise to ask your doctor's advice. Regular exercise helps to reduce high blood pressure and even if you've already had a heart attack moderate exercise will help strengthen your heart and may help you avoid another heart attack. If you've got a cold, flu, a sore throat, or a temperature, it's wise not to exercise until you feel better
- 'I feel fine'. How you feel is a good indication of your state of health, but it's not the whole story. You can feel well and have diseased coronary arteries. And no matter how well you feel, you'll feel *better* when you exercise regularly
- 'I'm too busy'. If you're not used to putting aside time to exercise, you may find it difficult to fit it in to a busy life. So assess your priorities: isn't maintaining your health and avoiding heart disease important for you?

Don't think of exercise as a chore; it will become a pleasure, and people who exercise regularly find that they're more relaxed and can cope more easily with work pressures and a busy life

- 'I'm not sporty'. You don't need to be: there are exercises to suit everyone. Even if you didn't play games at school, you can find an exercise you will enjoy. You don't have to reach championship level – or anywhere near it – to enjoy a sport and to get benefit from it
- 'Exercise is more likely to cause a heart attack than prevent one'. Of course some people will have a heart attack while jogging; but far more will have one lying in bed or sitting watching the television. Yet these pastimes are not considered dangerous.

If a middle-aged person, whose arteries are already partially clogged, suddenly starts taking vigorous exercise, he or she runs an increased risk of a heart attack. But built up gradually, exercise is not only safe, it will also help to protect you against a heart attack. Someone who dies jogging might have died even earlier if he hadn't exercised.

Remember, too, that just because you exercise and are fit, you don't have *carte blanche* to do whatever you want with your body. Smoking and eating fatty foods will still increase your risk of a heart attack

Slim while you sleep

People who are overweight don't necessarily eat more than those who are thin, it's just that they don't exercise as much. Different people do, of course, handle the same amount of food differently; their bodies burn it up at different rates. It's true, for instance, that you'd have to walk about three miles to burn off the calories from a large piece of chocolate cake, but if you exercise regularly, your body becomes more efficient at burning up calories so that even when you're resting your 'tickover' speed (or your 'basal metabolic rate') is increased. So you burn up calories more efficiently even as you sleep.

Also, if your food intake remains the same over a period of weeks or months of regular exercising, you're bound to lose weight. Slowly but surely, that's the best way to take the pounds off and make sure they keep off. For example, if you walked an extra mile a day, you'd lose a pound or so each month – a stone a year. That mile might take you twenty minutes to walk, but twenty one-minute walks would be just as effective for losing weight.

A myth about exercise is that it always increases the appetite. It doesn't; in fact, you may find that exercising before a meal actually curbs your appetite.

Getting started

If you're very unfit, or if it's a long time since you took any form of exercise, you should start increasing your physical activity gently and gradually before attempting any more vigorous activity. Here are some suggestions you can weave into your everyday life. (Even if you do exercise regularly two or three times a week, it would still help you if you could follow as many of the suggestions as you can.)

- walk to work or to the station, or try to walk part of the way
- park your car some distance from your destination and walk the rest of the way
- get off the bus one or two stops early and walk the rest of the way
- cycle to work
- use stairs instead of lifts wherever you can
- do some gardening or some more gardening. Mow the lawn more often
- think before you ever use your car: 'can I walk there?'

Walking

Walking, in fact, is one of the very best exercises and it's an excellent way to start exercising. Walking is safe for people of all ages and it can bring you the same benefits as more vigorous forms of exercise provided you do it for long enough and walk fast enough. Aim to get out of puff.

Build up slowly and aim for a twenty- or thirty-minute walk where you get out of breath but can still carry on a normal conversation. After a while, you'll want to walk for longer as you'll feel barely warmed up after twenty minutes, so increase the length of time you walk and try to walk part of the way uphill.

Something more vigorous

Once you're feeling fitter, you'll want to tackle some more vigorous exercise. If you're under thirty-five, you could start with this, but take it slowly and easily at first. Compared with walking, more vigorous exercise will get you fit faster and will take less time each day.

Even if you're fit, however, it's always wise to take it slowly for the first five minutes as you warm up. You should start with some gentle bending and stretching

Build up gradually

exercises. Most injuries and sprains are the result of overdoing it too quickly. Always 'cool down' as well, by walking or moving slowly for a few minutes after you've finished brisk exercise. A lot of your blood is sent to your legs to supply them with oxygen during exercise. When your muscles are working hard, they help to shift this blood back to the heart and brain. If you stop suddenly, the blood 'pools' in your legs, your brain doesn't get enough, and you may become dizzy.

After very heavy exercise, you may become dehydrated; it's wise to top up with clear fluids (which don't need to be sugary) after you've finished, and perhaps during exercise, too, if it's a hot day and you're sweating a lot.

Running or jogging These are really the same thing: a jog is a slow run. You can run at whatever speed suits you, and it will increase your level of fitness quickly and efficiently. Again, you need to go slowly for several months, at first alternately walking and jogging. Build up gradually and don't get too breathless. You're not in a race, so don't increase your speed until you're ready. The time you spend jogging is more important than the speed you jog at.

Try to run on grass whenever you can as it's easier on your feet. You do need to buy a good pair of running shoes: go to a specialist sports shop and ask for advice.

'I always run with a friend because it's fun, it's somebody to chat to, and if you're a fairly serious runner, which I am, on the bad days a kind of "buddy" system exists where you help each other through bad patches.'

LENNIE BENNETT – *comedian*

You'll get a lot of advice and help, too, if you join an athletics club. Jogging with a friend will also encourage you to do it on a regular basis and not to skip it if you don't feel like it on a particular day.

Swimming This is probably the ideal all-round exercise. It's good for people of all ages and all levels of physical fitness. It's especially good if you have joint problems or backache, or if you are overweight, as the water supports the weight of your body. It's something you can do with all the family, too, but splashing around at the shallow end with the kids doesn't count as aerobic exercise. To get the maximum benefit for your heart, you need to swim laps using one of the serious strokes: crawl, butterfly, backstroke, or breaststroke. Build up your stamina to the point where you can swim for twenty minutes without stopping.

Cycling Again, cycling may be a pleasant pastime for the whole family. To ensure you get aerobic exercise, though, you have to get your legs moving hard and rhythmically. Build up gradually, beginning with five minutes a week and increasing the length of time you cycle by weekly five-minute increments. Make sure you know your Highway Code, and wear reflective clothing at night.

Badminton, tennis, and squash Badminton and tennis can be fun to play even if you're a beginner, but the benefit to your heart increases as your play improves. Then the exercise each provides becomes more aerobic, with fewer stops and starts. Singles tennis is

'I try to play tennis at least three times a week with a pro, and once a day the rest of the time, if I can, with anyone who will play. If you play hard tennis you'll get everything pumping. I mean I come off absolutely bathed in sweat, and I feel that it must help. Certainly it makes me feel much better and I have much more stamina. I think exercise is great psychologically.'

CLIFF RICHARD

'I'm not playing professionally now and so I'm not quite as rigid on my regime, but I'm also very conscious, even more conscious, about being fit, about having a continual exercise program. As I look at the future, I realize that this physical fitness is not just for tennis but it's really for my whole life. I'll be more productive in anything that I do if I'm physically fit. I'll be more alert, I'll feel better about myself, and so I'm going to look in the future to keep myself fit and healthy.'

STAN SMITH – *Wimbledon champion*

likely to be more vigorous than doubles so is likely to bring you more benefit. Again, both can be family games, though they're less likely to be vigorous.

You should already be fit when you start playing squash; it can be a fast, hard game, but it is excellent for stamina. If you're over thirty-five when you start, make sure you begin by playing very gently.

Other games You can judge whether other games will help your cardiovascular fitness by considering if they get your large muscles moving rhythmically over a period of time, getting you breathless in the process. Obviously, rugby and soccer do (unless you're in goal) while cricket does not. Golf is decent exercise if you carry your own clubs and walk fast, but it's unlikely to provide you with vigorous exercise.

Dancing   Waltzing isn't going to do too much for your heart, though vigorous disco dancing may provide aerobic exercise. Aerobic dancing classes, however, do provide a way of getting exercise which is of benefit to the heart. Some of them have been criticized for pushing people too quickly and so causing injuries or sprains, but some people enjoy exercising in company and find it encourages them to keep going. If you begin gradually, aerobics classes are a good way of getting exercise.

'I've got one of those exercise bikes, rather than an ordinary bike, and I can really get some exercise going on that. If it's a nice day I take my bike in the garden. Or I go into the bathroom and have a pedal in the bathroom because there's plenty of room in there. It's not boring. I sometimes put my headphones on and start singing. While I'm pedalling, I could be learning my scripts in my mind, I could be listening to music.'

FAITH BROWN – *comedienne*

Indoor activities If you don't want to get out of breath in public, or if you're in a hotel room somewhere, you can still take exercise that is beneficial to your heart. Running on the spot and skipping with a rope will provide you with aerobic exercise. You may find it boring, but you could always listen to music at the same time. Repeatedly going up and down stairs will give you aerobic exercise, too. You need to take this easy, though, as it can very quickly raise your heart rate, so check your pulse. Stepping on and off a bench or block nine to twelve inches high will give you the same sort of beneficial exercise.

Stationary bikes and rowing machines will also give you good aerobic exercise. The best kinds of exercise bikes have adjustable resistance on the pedals so that you can work harder as you get fitter. Both   kes and rowing machines are excellent for getting and keeping fit. Again, the problem may be boredom. But you can watch television, listen to the radio, read, or have a conversation at the same time. This may be the solution if you have a very busy life and can't see where exercise would fit into it.

Keep exercising You don't need to stick to just one form of exercise; you can ring the changes. Whatever you decide to do, though, you must do it regularly. And you need to keep at it. Unfortunately, fitness isn't something you can put into a deposit account and draw out when you need it. You need to earn it, week by week. But once you begin to exercise regularly, you'll wonder why you didn't always do it.

HEART FACTS

Those who exercise regularly are less likely to get a heart attack; those who don't double their risk

★

Exercise reduces body fat, lowers blood pressure, strengthens the heart, relieves stress, decreases the level of blood cholesterol

★

The beneficial effects of exercise last much longer than the exercise itself

CHAPTER 7

OBESITY

If you're overweight, you're in good company: over half of the adult population in this country is overweight. Women admit that they are overweight more readily than men, who tend to think that their increased weight is normal for their age. It isn't. You are overweight if:

- you're more than 10lbs heavier than you were as a slim 20-year-old
- the roll of fat you can pinch at your waist is thicker than the width of your index finger

You can assess how overweight you are, and find your 'ideal' weight, by consulting the chart opposite. 'Ideal' weight for people of a particular height is that weight which is associated with the lowest death rate. It has nothing to do with how you look, though you will look and feel your best if you're around this ideal weight.

The risk to your heart

On its own, obesity only begins to add significantly to your risk of a heart attack when it is very great – perhaps four or five stone over your ideal weight. It is then very important for you to lose weight, and you should seek your doctor's advice.

◆

'I don't think healthy food is boring, not at all, in fact we have proven the opposite. It can be very exciting, creative, different, and fit for your heart, too! I have lost over six kilos, just like that, without eating less, just eating the right things. And it's not necessarily the most expensive food either. You can do something with cabbage, something with leeks: just simple basic ingredients. You can produce wonders with them.

ANTON MOSIMANN – *The Dorchester's head chef*

◆

But don't be complacent if you are only moderately overweight because you are likely to have some of the risk factors which, in turn, increase your odds of heart disease. People who are only slightly overweight – a couple of stone, perhaps – tend to have:

- higher blood pressure
- higher blood cholesterol
- a higher risk of having diabetes

Studies in the US have shown that weight control in the population might reduce the incidence of high blood pressure by up to fifty per cent. Losing weight also increases the 'good' cholesterol and decreases the 'bad' (see p. 43).

Control your weight

You should aim to get your weight down to within the ideal weight range. If you follow the advice in this book, your weight will return to within that range. You shouldn't aim for a drastic or quick weight loss; if you change your habits so that you lose weight steadily – perhaps a pound a month (which is nearly a stone a year) – it is more likely that your weight loss will be permanent.

Find Your Ideal Weight

Underweight.
Are you eating enough?

OK.
This is the desirable weight range for health.

Overweight.
Your health could suffer – don't get any fatter!

Fat.
It's important for you to lose weight.

Very fat.
This is severe and treatment is urgently required.

Your height in feet and inches (1 foot = approx 0.3 metres)

6'1 6' 5'11 5'10 5'9 5'8 5'7 5'6 5'5 5'4 5'3 5'2 5'1 5' 4'11

Your weight in stones (1 pound = approx 0.45 kilograms)

7 8 9 10 11 12 13 14 15 16 17 18 19 20 21 22 23

From J. S. Garrow's Treat Obesity Seriously published by Churchill Livingstone, Edinburgh (1981)

'I've lost five stone – I was drinking too much and I was eating the wrong things. For instance, I hardly ever ate fruit, but now I eat fruit, and I eat chicken, and fish; and nothing like as much red meat as I used to eat. I used to drink pints of milk when I got thirsty; that's all gone – it's all skimmed milk now. I feel so much better since I've taken myself firmly in control, I feel better than I have done for years. I know if I had stayed the same weight I was – nineteen stone – I would be gone by now.'

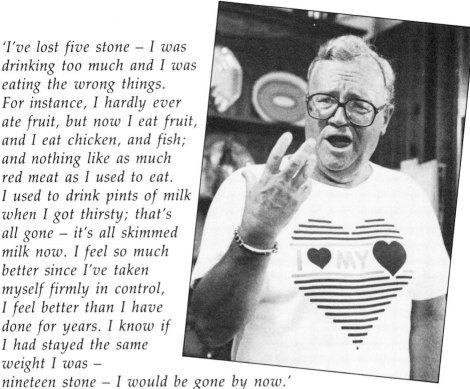

SIR HARRY SECOMBE

Diet You don't need to go on a special diet to lose weight. If you follow the dietary guidelines for avoiding a heart attack you will lose weight, or maintain your weight at a healthy level. Remember that fat and sugar pack a lot of calories into a small space. You're overweight because you're eating too much of those two things.

No one needs to feel hungry while losing weight. If you are trying to follow a 'diet' in which you're not getting enough to eat, and which makes you hungry, you're going to find it extremely difficult to stick to it. And you will be tempted to binge. At the very least, you're going to torment yourself fantasizing about all the food you can't have, so why not eat your fill of the food you *can* have? Food with complex carbohydrates – starches and fibre – is filling, remember, without being fattening. So wholemeal bread (without butter or jam), potatoes (not cooked in fat), and fresh fruit will satisfy your appetite without your taking in too many calories.

Remember that alcohol, too, delivers many calories per sip! Many people who are overweight would lose weight if they reduced their alcohol consumption.

Exercise Our ancestors ate more calories than we do but weighed less because they were more active. The exercise chapter tells you how to slim while you sleep: if you exercise regularly, your body's tickover rate increases and you burn up calories more efficiently.

The best way of losing weight is always a two-pronged attack: watch what you're eating and start to take more exercise. Exercise will also start turning your flab into muscle. So you'll look better even before the results show up on your bathroom scales. Remember, too, that regular exercise will help to control your appetite.

Smoking Don't say: 'If I've got to lose weight, I'd better carry on smoking.' It's not inevitable that you'll put on weight if you stop smoking: only a third of people do. And you don't need to join them if you watch what you eat and start exercising when you give up. If you are overweight, it is all the more important that you stop smoking.

HEART FACTS

Over half the adult population in Britain is overweight

★

Being overweight can increase the odds of a heart attack in several different ways

★

Most people are overweight because they eat too much fat and sugar

★

By following the advice in this book, it is possible to reduce weight without starving and bingeing

★

Losing weight will lower blood pressure, lower blood cholesterol, lower the risk of diabetes and lower the risk of a heart attack

★

CHAPTER 8

STRESS AND PERSONALITY

Many people would mention 'stress' first when asked to list the causes of heart disease. But, in fact, the medical evidence does not bear this out in relation to the other risk factors. This is partly because of the problem of knowing exactly what stress is. Most of us might think we know it when we feel it, but we'd be hard pressed to define it. One man's stress may be another's impetus for achieving things in life, so it's impossible for anyone to assess how stressful a job is for the particular individual who does it.

Incidentally, the idea of the high-powered business executive being the prime candidate for a heart attack is rather outdated. Of course, such people do get heart attacks. Anyone can get a heart attack. But manual workers are now more often prime candidates for heart disease. (Perhaps because they have more of the other risk factors.)

Natural reactions to natural stress

The body has a natural reaction to stress. In the days when stress might be caused by an attacking predator, the body was prepared for a rapid retreat by the stress hormones, like adrenalin, which were pumped into the blood. If the enemy was small scale, the same reaction would tone the body up for a fight. Adrenalin increases the heart rate, pushes up the blood pressure, and causes the blood vessels in the skin to contract in order to make more blood available for the muscles. It's also responsible for giving us that feeling of 'nerves', with sweaty palms and butterflies in the tummy. The body is then keyed up and ready for 'fight or flight'.

Reactions to other stress

The same reaction, the outpouring of adrenalin, occurs when we get angry, tense, frightened, or excited. So when we drive in the rush-hour, have an argument, or watch our favourite football team lose yet again, the level of stress hormones in our body goes up. The stress hormones are

'Stress is very important. I'm a great believer in mind over matter and in being at peace with yourself, and being happy. I've never believed that you can divorce the mind from the body; when I was a doctor I never thought that. So I am concerned about the pace of life and perhaps that's always been one of the reasons why I've been one of those who is very reluctant to make Sunday just another day. I personally find tremendous strength from being able to switch off on a Sunday and keep it very much for my family. I have to be persuaded very hard to do any political activity on a Sunday, and it's not just on religious grounds – although that's a view you should respect – but on psychological ones. You should take one day, at least, where the stresses are not so great, where you don't go through the normal routine, and I think that's important today.'

RT HON. DR DAVID OWEN, MP

neutralized by exercise, but, of course, when we're impatiently sitting in traffic, they continue to circulate in the bloodstream. It's thought these hormones may over time increase the risk of a heart attack by raising the blood pressure and the level of cholesterol and so accelerating the furring-up of the arteries. It's probably chronic stress over a period of months or years that is the main culprit: stress caused by problems at work, money worries, family arguments, loneliness, or unemployment.

Several studies have shown that people who change jobs frequently have more chance of a heart attack than those who stay in the same job. Work in the United States has also shown that men who move from rural areas to work in large cities greatly increase their risk of heart disease compared with those who remain in the country.

But some people thrive on stress, enjoying the challenge of being under pressure and giving of their best when they are. Others collapse under stress and are unable to cope with what seem like insignificant pressures. This means that the whole question of stress is still under investigation. People under the most intense pressures can still escape heart disease while those who seem to live carefree lives end up getting heart attacks. It seems that it's not so much the pressures we're under, but how we respond to them that matters. And that brings us to personality.

Personality types

Over the last twenty years, research has shown that there are particular personality types who seem more likely to have a heart attack. These have been called 'type A'; those who are less likely to develop heart disease are labelled 'type B'.

TYPE A PERSONALITIES
- are striving and ambitious
- are competitive
- demand perfection of themselves and others
- always feel and act rushed; are always pressed for time
- are impatient and let small frustrations get to them
- find it hard to forget their worries and to relax
- eat fast and talk fast
- interrupt others and finish their sentences if they hesitate for a word
- give the impression of trying to do too many things at once

TYPE B PERSONALITIES
- are the opposite of type As
- are easy-going, and philosophical
- take everything in their stride
- find it easy to relax and switch off
- don't feel they have to do everything to perfection
- enjoy the present moment

'I smoked a hundred a day and, like all smokers, kidded myself that I needed it for my nerves. My nerves got progressively worse and I smoked more and more, and in the end I realized I stank, the children stank of it, the house stank of it, I couldn't taste my food. I'd get up at three in the morning to go to a fag machine in the street in my pyjamas, things like that. Then I thought, I've got to give this up, this is insanity.'

SPIKE MILLIGAN

Of course, these are rather rough and ready classifications. The vast majority of us have both A and B characteristics, either of which can be expressed, depending on the circumstances we're in. So classifying people in this way is not like measuring something scientific and accurate – such as taking their blood pressure or their pulse. But when people are assigned by psychologists into one or other category, it is remarkable that type As consistently seem more prone to heart attacks, other risk factors being equal. Some studies have show that being a type A personality doubles the risk of a heart attack.

If you recognize yourself as falling in the type A category, it certainly doesn't mean that you are inevitably in line for a heart attack. It's vitally important for you, though, to ensure you tackle every other risk. If you've decided you are type B, don't be too complacent, either. Even the most placid person can get a heart attack. You still need to reduce the other risks, too.

How *not* to cope with stress

The great danger of feeling under stress is that it may push you into behaviour which will increase the chance of a heart attack. So stress could cause you to smoke, to eat more, or to drink more. Indeed, this may be the very reason why those who can't cope with stress have an increased risk of heart disease. It's not so much the stress itself which is increasing the risk, but rather the behaviour it provokes.

- don't smoke more
- don't eat more
- don't drink more
- don't abandon exercise
- don't drink endless cups of coffee (caffeine is a stimulant and increases tension)
- *do* learn to relax

Stress is an inevitable, and perhaps even essential, part of life. You need to counter it by finding ways to relax.

Coping with stress

When under stress, don't fly off the handle or, worse, bottle up your frustration and tension. There are a number of ways, both mental and physical, to work stress out of your system.

Exercise

This is one of the best ways of relieving stress and easing away tensions. The feelings of well-being and relaxation

*'Stress is part of the job but while you run you
really do feel relaxed, even if the stress returns
twenty minutes after you've had a shower. The fact is,
while you're running, while you're exercising, and
while you're having a shower, the stressful aspects go
away.'*

RT HON. NEIL KINNOCK, MP

brought on by exercise last much longer than the actual time you spend exercising. And this is, of course, the natural way of coping with those stress hormones. Exercise shouldn't be too vigorous at first, but even short walks are a good way of relaxing and releasing tension (see chapter 5).

Get to know yourself

Next time you get angry, tense, or frustrated, engage yourself in an inner conversation. For example, if you are stuck in traffic and are going to be late for an important meeting, ask yourself why you are getting fraught. Tell yourself that there's nothing you can do about the situation. You may as well have ten minutes of calm rather than ten minutes of seething anger. Think of the extra time as a bonus, a gift. Listen to the radio; plan your next holiday; imagine what you'd do if your premium bond came up.

You might find it useful to write down the situations in which you get particularly tense, angry, or frustrated. Try to analyse why you react in those ways. Think either of ways you can avoid those situations or of arguments you can use in your inner conversation to calm yourself down. A feeling for the absurd and a sense of humour help.

Deep breathing

This sounds a very simple technique, but slow, deep breaths are an effective way of calming down. Sit quietly and close your eyes. Breathe slowly through your nose, trying to take in the air down to your toes. Then slowly and steadily breathe out again. Concentrate on observing your breathing. If your mind races to something else, bring it back to concentrate on the breaths. A couple of minutes of this is guaranteed to relax you.

Relax the body

This is a way of getting your muscles to relax, eliminating feelings of tension. Sit comfortably in an upright chair. Press your feet firmly onto the ground, clenching the muscles in your feet and legs as you do so. Do this for about ten seconds and then let go. Feel the tension draining out of your legs. Now hold your arms up with your elbows bent and clench your fists, clenching all the muscles in your arms, too. Do this for ten seconds and then let go. Feel the tension draining out of your arms. Rest your hands gently on your lap. You can repeat this with your legs and arms a couple of times. Then sit still and take some deep breaths.

Meditation   You can get yourself in the frame of mind to meditate by using the deep-breathing and muscle-relaxing exercises. Then you can try one of several techniques. You could focus your mind on a soothing image like gentle waves on the seashore or leaves rustling in the wind. You could concentrate on your normal breathing, just by being aware of it and coming back to it if other thoughts intrude. You might repeat to yourself 'in . . . .out' as you breathe. Most religions use similar techniques in prayer: repeating a mantra in Hinduism or the 'Jesus' prayer in Christianity. Repeat a word or phrase to yourself, bringing your mind back to it when it wanders. Relax into the steady rhythm of it for five or ten minutes.

Recent medical research has shown that this sort of meditation or prayer not only makes you feel more relaxed and less tense but also actually helps to lower your blood pressure. Patients who have had mild hypertension and who have been taught to practise this technique were found to be able to reduce their blood pressure without the aid of drugs.

HEART FACTS

Stress hormones, like adrenalin, may push up blood pressure and blood cholesterol when they are not neutralized by exercise

———————— ★ ————————

Stress can cause you to smoke, eat and drink more and so increase several risk factors

———————— ★ ————————

CHAPTER 9

CONCLUSION

Everybody in Britain is at risk of a heart attack; everybody can reduce that risk, and the plan of action at the end of the book should help you and your family. You can't be too young and you're never too old to follow the heart disease avoidance advice outlined in this book.

Starting young

Remember that the foundation of heart disease is laid in childhood. Fit young adults have been shown to have the beginning of the furring-up process of the coronary arteries. You need to ensure that you aren't increasing the risk of your children having a heart attack in later life. You don't only hand on genes to your children; you set them an example and a pattern for life. Make sure it's a healthy one.

Smoking

Children are more likely to smoke if they have parents who smoke. You can scarcely complain if your children follow an example you have set, and there can be very strong peer-group pressure on children to smoke. Remember an anti-smoking ten-year-old can become a regular smoker by the age of fourteen. You need to discuss the question of smoking with your children openly, without nagging them. Discussion before they are likely to be smokers means they are better prepared to make informed decisions and not follow the crowd.

Diet and obesity

Fat children usually have fat parents. Unhealthy eating habits are passed down from one generation to another. The advice about fat, sugar, fibre, and salt applies just as much to children as to adults. It *is* possible to bring children up preferring chicken drumsticks to hamburgers, and apples to bars of chocolate. It *is* possible to encourage children not to develop a taste for salty food by steering them away from crisps and salted snacks. It is difficult, but it's worth trying. Unfortunately, school meals are usually a disaster area. Complain to the education authority if healthy choices are not available.

*'What I want to do is make my children healthy.
So I learnt more about healthy food, and, in
particular, how to avoid heart disease. That
meant a diet with much less fat in it, especially
saturated animal fat, less sugar, and more fibre.
We now eat many more vegetables and much
more fruit that we used to eat. And I discovered
that, if I could teach my children how to eat
healthily right from the start, eating the right diet
would eventually become a habit – they would
assume that yoghurt is a suitable kind of thing to
eat for a pudding, for instance. I do think that the
influence of what one does at home is terribly
important and can affect how your children eat
and what kind of adults they'll eventually become.'*

CAROLINE WALDEGRAVE – *cookery writer*

If you are thinking of making changes in the way you eat, involve the children in the discussion. Get them to help you to make changes and stick to your resolutions. Setting the family goals (and giving yourself rewards) should prove effective.

Involve your children in the decisions you make in the supermarket and encourage them to help you to read food labels. Teach them what to look for and what to avoid. If you make it a game they will enjoy searching for the healthy foods and avoiding the unhealthy.

Exercise If exercise is a normal part of your life it will become that in your children's lives, too. You can bring your children up to think that physical activity is normal, or you can bring them up to think that lying in front of the television is the most relaxing way to spend leisure time. Set a good example.

If you've had a heart attack The advice in this book still applies to you even if you have had a heart attack. You should take action on each of the risks to stop yourself from getting another. A heart attack will have given you a chance to stand back and assess your life.

- blood pressure. Your doctor should be keeping a check on your blood pressure. If it's high, he may treat it with tablets, but look at the chapter on blood pressure again to see what you can do for yourself
- diet. The advice in the diet chapter should be followed, particularly on fats and fibre, and you should aim to get to your ideal weight
- smoking. You're heading for certain and imminent death if you continue to smoke after a heart attack or if you have angina. You must stop
- exercise. Don't feel you're an invalid after a heart attack. Take regular exercise, starting very gently. Your doctor will advise you. You can get back to a normal, active life after a heart attack.
- stress. Assess your personality and how you react to stress. Learn how to cope with it.

There's good evidence that if you take action on these points, you'll reduce your risk of getting another heart attack. It's never too late to reduce that risk.

A plan of action

It's impossible to predict with complete accuracy whether or not you will get a heart attack, but by now you will have quite a good idea of the risks you are running.

- go back through the book and write down all the risks you are taking that make a heart attack more likely. You could do a list for each member of your family
- remember that the biggest risks are smoking, high blood pressure, and high blood cholesterol
- if you don't know your blood pressure, remember to ask your doctor to take it next time you visit the surgery. You could ask for your blood cholesterol to be taken too
- as you go through the book again, write down all the changes you could make in your lifestyle. Note which are changes for the family as a whole and which are for you personally
- discuss the changes you are going to make as a family. You may find it useful to make a 'contract' which everyone signs. If you're asking people to make changes – particularly children – you need to think of a system of rewards
- put the changes you're going to make in an order of priorities. If you smoke, smoking should top your list. Other changes you may make in any order you wish, but don't try to do too many things at once. If you make

changes slowly and gradually, they are more likely to become incorporated into your normal life

● work out a rough timetable for your order of priorities. You don't need to stick to it rigidly, but it's important to have one so you see things in perspective. For example:

April–change to wholemeal bread
May–change to semi-skimmed milk

is more realistic than:

Monday–change to skimmed milk
Tuesday–stop adding salt to food

To make all the changes you've listed might take a couple of years

● put your proposed changes in your diary or write them on a calendar. Check your progress in one month, three months, six months and one year

Don't break your heart

Health education is about choice. You've now got the information you need to make an informed decision about how you personally can reduce your risk of a heart attack. You have to be convinced enough to make the changes; no one can force you into them. The decision to make them is a crucial part of being able to carry them out. It's your choice. But then it's your heart.

Index